INFLUENCE
What's the Missing Piece?

Karen Keller, Ph.D.

EPI

Executive Press, Inc.

Book design and layout by: Zachary Cole - Chisik Studio
Interior designs by: Brittney Owens

Printed in the United States of America.
First Edition: July 2017

Library of Congress Cataloging-in-Publication Data

Keller, Ph.D, Karen
Influence: What's the missing piece? / Karen Keller, Ph.D.

Hardcover ISBN: 978-0-9991668-1-9
Paperback ISBN: 978-0-9991668-0-2
ebook ISBN: 978-0-9991668-2-6

ADDITIONAL PRAISE FOR

INFLUENCE
What's the Missing Piece?

"Dr. Keller's ideas about influence are the exact opposite of what we have been taught. Dr. Keller's insights show that business success is no longer only about the bottom line, but more about the influential culture that supports the organization." **Rose Putnam – PepsiCo**

"I found the KII® to be insightful and useful. My clients are in leadership positions who regularly ask themselves, "Am I being influential and effective?" The Keller Influence Indicator® clearly gives them areas to work on and is an extremely powerful tool. The KII® adds value to the coaching profession as a whole." **Mark Smith, ACC – Wildcats Adventure Coaching, Johannesburg, South Africa**

"Two things are immediately noticed in executive coaching with Dr. Keller: (1) her expertise and (2) insight on the value of productive team performance, decision making, and influence mastery. Our division saw a 51% increase in shared leadership, a 57% increase in enhanced team competency, and a 64% increase in developing measureable performance targets. This overwhelmingly contributed to a 46% increase in our continued enrollment from the previous year." **Deb Conklin, Ph.D. – Former Executive Director Continuing Education Indiana-Purdue University**

"The Keller Influence Indicator® (KII®) has passed the 'thump' test – it is 50 pages of information, ideas, and knowledge about me – my competitive advantage, blindspots and areas for improvement. The KII® would benefit the C-Suite tremendously from finding out how influential they can be, what they could be doing better and how they could leverage their influence traits. The KII® can help from the CEO to the new manager to the sales team in improving their ability to influence their environment, relationships, and self, as well as enhance their leadership ability." **Jean Kelley – Industrial Sociologist and Author "Look. Leap. Lead. A Pocket Guide to Being a Memorable Leader" Tulsa, Oklahoma**

"Dr. Keller's influence strategies and materials helped me secure a position as a Vice President in an international company with annual sales of 1.3 billion. This move was a 25% increase in salary with a sizeable career promotion. Dr. Keller understands the dynamics of the highly competitive and political environments, and possesses the practical experience and 'know-how' which motivates her clients to achieve great success." **Steve Miller – (ret.) Global VP Supply Chain Management Wabash National Inc.**

To my husband and favorite person,
Randall Rider,
and to my two emerging influencers,
Beth and Megan

The FIRST requirement for being an influential person in all aspects of your life is to know yourself. The second requirement is to show the world.

- DR. KAREN KELLER

CONTENTS

What You Will Find
In This Book

Influence is not difficult once you understand the path to being influential first. Only then is when you can become a great influencer. Here's a brief overview of what this primer on influence entails.

Chapter 1 explains the difference between having influence and being influential, why this difference is critical to understand, and how it will differentiate you from being an influencer to being a great influencer.

Chapter 2 sets the stage that influence and success depend on the organization AND the employee. A person cannot expect to show up for work and be handed influence. Every employee must bring their best to the job and in doing so will find that when they deliver what the organization needs, their own needs will be met as well.

Chapter 3 introduces the four organizational needs that people have to meet to experience a fulfilling work life: recognition, participation, transformation, and connection. This chapter clarifies what makes these four needs a significant part of organizational success, as well as how they are a defining piece of creating the influential organization.

Chapter 4 explains why and how a person meets their six basic human needs: certainty, uncertainty/variety, significance, love and connection, growth, and contribution. You must understand the significance of meeting these needs and how it lends to a high-performing influential employee, executive, or CEO.

Chapter 5 brings Chapter 3 and Chapter 4 together. It lays out the plan for organizations and individuals to formulate a mutually supportive way of working together for the benefit of everyone, including the success of the company. Doing this well results in a thriving organization that delivers on its promises without sacrificing the authenticity and integrity of every member.

Chapter 6 raises the awareness and importance of employee identity which is formed by the alignment of personal core values and organizational goals. Employee identity is formed through intention, purpose, and ownership. Developing one's personal brand drives company growth and supports company vision. In this chapter the relationship between human needs and teams is illustrated.

Chapter 7 introduces the Seven Influence Traits®: confidence, commitment, courage, passion, empowering, trustworthiness, and likeability. These traits are the cornerstone of being influential. They make up the foundation for every great conversation, relationship, and success – big or small. In this chapter you will discover what it looks like when you are deficient in these traits and the impact it has on others, your team, and the organization.

Chapter 8 explains the Keller Influence Indicator® (KII®), the instrument that measures each of the Seven Influence Traits® and gives you a benchmark of where you are with each of these traits. The KII® is the only statistically proven valid instrument that measures influence potential. It identifies emerging leaders, high potentials, and missing resources. The KII® is the anchor for the KII® Programs which are designed to identify areas of power, influence, and human capital assets according to the strength and maximization of the Seven Influence Traits®. This tool prepares an organization's internal environment and culture for unforeseen opportunities and continued prosperity.

Chapter 9 shows that the way to achieve the highest degree of influence, trust, and engagement is developing people through the lens of being influential. This chapter covers the personal and organizational benefits to building people's influence potential. There is a difference between who you are and who you've learned to be. This difference is critical to understand when becoming an influential person.

Chapter 10 discusses The Five Organizational Competencies™: leadership, communication, team effectiveness, strategy/solutions, and execution/evaluation and how they are impacted by the Seven Influence Traits®. These five competencies have been identified as the most critical areas of skill development and behavioral change in an organization.

Chapter 11 ties everything together. Influence is the "make or break" factor and we have not been fully in tune with how being influential is not the same as having influence AND that we all can learn how to become influential. We can stop DOING and begin BEING. By understanding the traits that affect being influential, the fact that we all possess these traits, and that we all can master them is the paradigm shift that takes a person and an organization to unprecedented levels of success. The good news is it's never too late.

Chapter 12 wraps up with going back to the whole premise for my research and this book: What could we accomplish if we knew more about our own potential for success, for leadership, for impacting others? Becoming influential, the missing piece to influence, starts with knowing your influence potential (KII®) and learning how to maximize each of the Seven Influence Traits®. With simple focus, you can increase your level of influence and your success in ALL areas of your life.

And lastly, you will find at the beginning of each chapter a visual roadmap showing the salient points and takeaways in that chapter. You can use this space to guide your thought process, make notes to yourself, and record ideas that occur for you.

Now, let's begin...

INFLUENCE
What's the Missing Piece?

Karen Keller, Ph.D.

Introduction

Father Antony (Tony) Fernando, a close family friend, was the priest at St. Mary's Catholic Church, where Mother Teresa of Calcutta (Kolkata) attended Mass. Although I never met Mother Teresa in person, I feel as if I got to know her through Father Tony. Among the many stories he shared, one in particular stood out for me, showing the influence of this woman who lived every day impacting the poorest of the poor and the richest of the rich.

During the 1970's, Mother Teresa noticed an office building in downtown Calcutta that was owned and used by the Communist Party in India. On the streets in front of this building were many homeless and dying people who had no place to go. Mother Teresa noticed there was empty space under the stairwell inside the building. She approached the caretaker of the building asking if she could bring a few people in at night to have protection from the weather. She said they would not be in the way and the stairwell could accommodate "just a few." After a week went by, Mother Teresa noticed there was an empty office space in the building. Once again, she approached the caretaker asking if she could use the office space at night for more people who were living on the street. The caretaker said okay.

Another week went by. Mother Teresa mentioned to the caretaker that at night most of the offices were empty and the workers were gone home. She asked if she could bring in the homeless and sick children to lay down in the hallways and offices, saying, "We'll be gone in the morning." Within two months, the people in the office building had made room during the day for the work Mother Teresa was doing for the homeless children. After six months, the Communist Party moved out and signed the building over to her to use for her work. The home Mother Teresa "found" is called the Shishu Bhavan (Home for the Children). How did this and so much more happen for this woman? She had no "influence" but she absolutely was influential.

Mother Teresa is known for her compassion but what about her courage, her confidence, and her commitment? Those characteristics factor into your level of influence. Have you ever thought about your own mastery of these traits? Have you ever wondered how someone becomes so influential and how you can have more influence?

Most people tend to ignore the obvious, mainly because it is obvious. In the search for success and happiness, they mistakenly overlook the basics. This book brings you back to the basics, the basics for *being influential.* You will learn how to become an influential leader, to be a more vital member of your team, and to ensure your ideas see the light of day within your organization.

The same tools of influence used by Mother Teresa, Gandhi, Mandela, Jesus Christ, and so many others to create world-wide phenomena are the same tools used by organizations to create breakthroughs in their industry. Organizations need influential people. To lead the change in business today, you need to think, act, and feel as an influencer and master your potential to influence. How do the most prosperous organizations do this? By developing their people to become influential.

In the movie, *Teacher's Pet,* Clark Gable played a seasoned, hard-nosed, 8th grade educated newspaper editor who knocks heads with an educated, Doris Day, the journalism instructor. Gable attends her class under the ruse of being a wallpaper salesman who wants to learn to write. While sitting in the class where he learns about the complexities and nuances of writing for a newspaper, he impresses the teacher. He writes his own article. He boils it down to the six important questions every news story should answer: who, what, where, when, how, and why. Gable said, "That's what tells the story. That's what connects the reader." He goes back to the basics. He also understands the importance of connection. Connection is the cornerstone of what it means to be influential.

This book takes you back to the basics to increase your level of influence success. Those basic building blocks are: confidence, commitment, courage, passion, empowering, trustworthiness, and likeability. In my research, I discovered these are the seven foundational pieces for every aspect of life and I created an instrument that measures these seven traits, the *Keller Influence Indicator® (KII®).* You might think, "My company doesn't care if I'm likeable or passionate. I'm just expected to do my job." Or, "My job description is about getting things done." Or, "My team is only interested in building strategy but getting it executed is the hard part." And this may be true. *Yet the most valuable resource you bring to your work and to your organization is your ability to be influential.* To get your work done, to perform your role, to do more than your title, to make a difference in output relies on how you influence yourself, your team, your peers, and your customers.

Not understanding the foundation of influence leads to frustration, fleeting success, and a total drain of your energy. When you tap in to your influence potential, the opposite occurs. Things fall into place for you, your success is lasting, and you feel energetic. You inspire others around you.

As people have read and commented on what I have written, blogged, and published on the subject of influence, the first question they ask is, "What made you do this?" The answer is simple: I wanted to give people a way to bring back into their lives and to the work environment what they need to live a life of happiness and community. In my work over the last several decades I have come to understand that is the bottom line for truly successful individuals and organizations. The question I asked myself was, "What needs to happen in order for us to be our best and do our best (and feel our best)?" And my answer was *become influential.*

My research took me back to the basics: human nature and common sense. When we get back to the basics of what we humans need and how we accomplish our goals, it all comes back to how strong we are in the seven identified traits listed above. If you think you are influential already, wonderful. You will go deeper to see just how influential you truly are. If you know you could use some improvement in your power to influence, you are in the right place.

This book was written for you if you have never raised your hand, didn't share an idea, stepped back into the crowd, and never heard your voice. It is for people who have the burning desire within themselves to make a difference, take charge, bring forth a new path, and create a better way of working together. This book is for you, right here, right now.

In these pages you'll find the tools to master your way of making a difference, of bringing your best to the table, and of being an asset to your company. These tools will motivate you in changing your company culture to one that nurtures the interaction and engagement among people, a culture that respects people's personal and organizational needs and supports a mutual agreement to meet those needs.

There are two things that change your life: one, you wait for something new to come into your life, to make it better, OR two, you say I want something new and go after it. Being an influencer has to come from you. You can become a more confident person, more committed, more courageous, but the decision to go for it is up to you. And your time is now.

This may be the most valuable information and know-how you may ever learn. These traits are the raw rubrics of having influence and being influential, and once you know them you can apply them to your work and business challenges.

We spend more time working than any other single activity in our lives. Work is the place that expects the most from us but often where we receive the least. But when you become influential in your work, you find your inspired spirit, and you can transform and impact the lives of those around you. Being influential affects every single aspect of your life, personally and professionally. The keys to making this shift are in your grasp. It is time to discover your influential self.

CHAPTER 1

Are You Influential?

Having Influence vs Being Influential

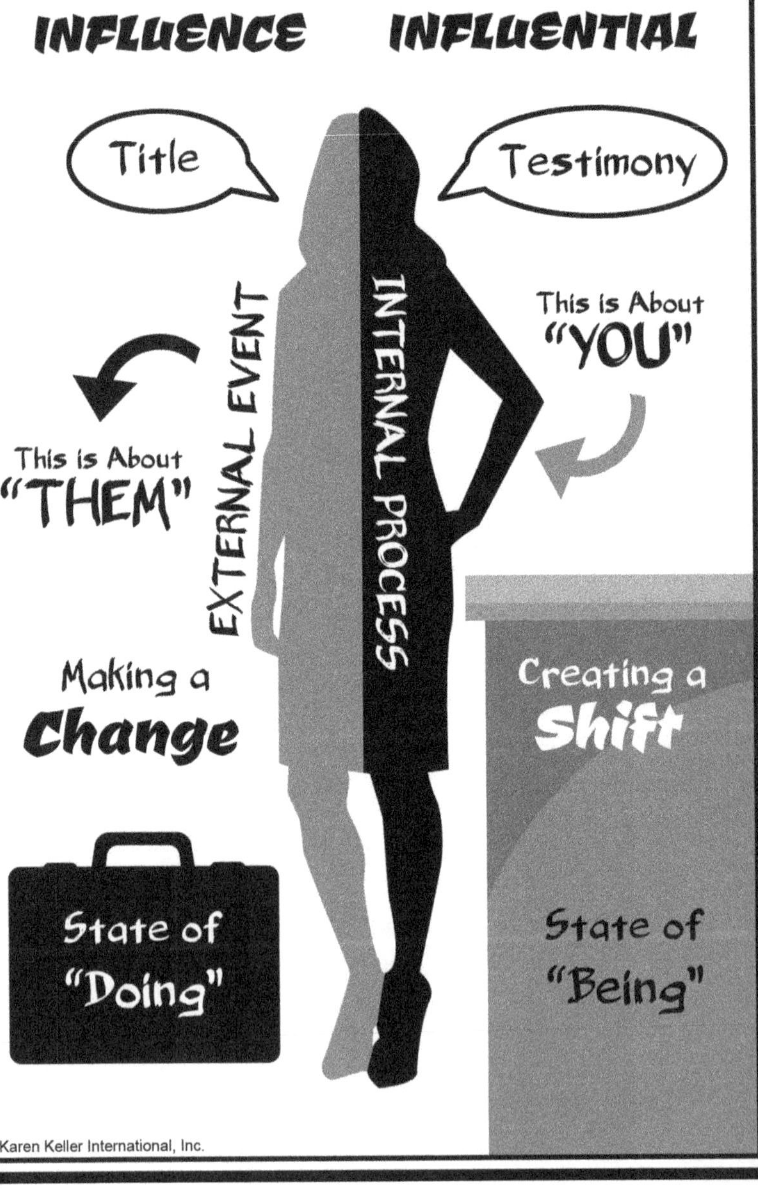

Are You Influential?

Let him that would move the world, first move himself.

- SOCRATES

Either you're influential or you're not. If you find yourself somewhere in between these two states, you still aren't influential - yet.

Influence is not about power. It's not about compliance. It's not about agreement. Influence is about connection. It's about integrity. It's about how you show up. Influence is present in every conversation, every action, every thought, and every feeling. It is everywhere.

Rob wanted to make a difference at work. In fact, he was expected to make a difference. After all, Rob was hired to bring change to the company. He had the necessary talent and skills to forge a surge of growth, but no one would listen to him. Rob tried everything he knew to pave the way for the company to understand what needed to be done. He talked to everyone, his boss, his team, and coworkers. The company ignored, avoided, resisted, and put the kibosh on most of Rob's best ideas.

After months of disappointment, Rob became tired and frustrated with poor performance, people complaining about each other, and the company pep talks each month (sugarcoat as he called it) about how "wonderful" things were going. Every idea he had was either shot down, or worse, others took credit. It seemed to be a never-ending cycle of go to work, tackle the same issues and problems, the same dysfunction, using the same, what the front office called "resources", only to be blamed for getting the same results. The expectation to create change was on top of Rob's day-to-day tasks that constantly piled up on his desk. Rob's story has enough experiences to fill a library of Dilbert comic strips. One day Rob simply had enough. He quit.

Does Rob sound all too familiar to you? Will he fare better elsewhere? Or is there something he could do differently? Something the company could do differently?

Are you wanting to make a difference in your position or company and have no idea where to start? You're not alone. Many organizations today are simply lost. Relationships are neglected, response to change is poor, and there is little appreciation for diversity of ideas and thought. Attempts to develop people do not address foundational issues. Generations are not listening to each other. And the list goes on.

The U.S. spends more than $365 billion annually on training and development yet something is still missing. All that money spent and employees are still stressed, sick, depressed and poor communicators. Results are the same-old same-old. People like Rob, who are energetic, imaginative, who want to move forward, who want to create a healthy culture, get fed up and quit. And the bottom line is not showing any improvement.

Companies go from one quick fix to another in effort to "fix" what is wrong. But most of them don't know what is really missing. As an executive coach and consultant, I've observed over the years this tornado of constant expectation of "fix, fix, fix this person." Organizations developed the mentality that a person needed to be fixed and if it didn't happen in three weeks, that person was gone! Now, thank goodness, much of that mindset has changed, however, how people are developed inside an organization still seriously needs to improve. If it doesn't, the Robs of the world (the most talented) will be lost to sinking organizations forever.

This is just one of the painful "truths" of the corporate world. But there is hope. What is the one thing that can make a difference? What will move a company from potential extinction to prosperity?

INFLUENCE.

Not the customary traditional definition and methods of influence. Businesses have for too long now believed that influence is the practices of what they "do" to people. They persuade them. They negotiate with them. They manipulate them. They intimidate them. They coerce them. They use tips, tricks, and tactics. These might be effective, for the short term, and need to be used ethically, but all these tips, tricks, and tactics need constant reinforcement. This kind of influence brings to mind that never-ending hamster wheel. The influencer must constantly be saying something or doing something in order to get what he or she wants. The influencer is always plotting and pondering what they must

DO. *I must persuade them. I must redirect their focus. I must move them to action.*

For centuries, "influence" has been defined as what you do, mainly to another person, to get what you want. The marketing industry has perfected this dynamic. They create a specific perception to get someone to purchase a product, attend an event, or start wearing purple lipstick. "Influence" is an attempt to move a person to do something by appealing to their emotions, instilling fear, or creating a sense of urgency. To create lasting healthy change in an organization however takes more than that.

Influencing people is about more than using the right arguments, a certain tone of voice, or a negotiation tactic. True influence is not about using tactics at all. And influence is not the exclusive property of those in the C-suite. "Coaching up," or the act of influencing people above you, is perhaps one of the most artful and powerful tools in business. Influence is for everyone.

Influence has customarily been associated with power, occurring when another person has such power or control or authority over a person, situation, or outcome. That is the defining characteristic of the traditional teachings of influence, that it is power in action—the power to control and cajole others into reaching a final, desired goal.

It's time to create a new definition. There is a better, longer-lasting solution. It's not about influence as we have been programmed to think of it; it's about developing people to BE INFLUENTIAL.

What Is "REAL" Influence?

Think of Mother Teresa or Gandhi or Martin Luther King,

Jr. or perhaps your favorite teacher or coach. They didn't use influence tactics or power plays – they were influential. The only true and lasting way to have influence is to BE influential.

Impacting people has to come from the heart, backed up with ethical intention and sincere motivation. True impact - real influence - has to involve connection and relationship. You (and your organization) can learn how to do just that. Whether it's in the form of marketing, sales, sports, leadership, business, or family, **influence is the cornerstone of all human interaction.**

The influence industry is exploding. Our society is flooded with suggestions and examples of compliance, persuasion, brainwashing, propaganda, and reframing all designed to help people get, do or be something more in their lives. Dr. Kelton Rhoads, founder of *Working Psychology,* estimates, "influence can be divided into at least 160 dimensions—and the list is growing."

What all these influence dimensions have in common is they are "externally based." They teach you to influence by doing or saying something to get a response. That puts you in a state of constant "doing." Think about the different types of influences that you experience every day—you might not even recognize them as influence in action—persuasion, manipulation, intimidation, negotiation, or coercion. Perhaps you know someone at work who can convince the boss that *anything* is a good idea, even if you know it's not. Or maybe you've known a few trendsetters in your day, such as the first person in your office to cut her hair a certain way or wear the latest fashions, and then the entire office follows suit.

No matter what your position in your company or family, you are influenced by everyone around you and you have influence on everyone, too. Real influence isn't about making others bend to your will. Influence is about achieving a goal either with or through another person or group of people while staying true to your own moral code. It may involve listening to others, having a certain conversation at just the right time, creating opportune moments yourself, involving others in a dialogue about a key decision, or simply dropping someone a quick note about an upcoming project or your big idea for a major client.

Influence is the foundation of all leadership success from the top to the bottom, no matter the organization, industry, or company. Up to this point, research has addressed ONLY a very particular aspect of influence:

How to get someone to **do what you want** them to do.
How to get someone to s**ay what you want** them to say.
How to get someone to **change what they feel.**
How to get someone to **change their beliefs.**

I've found the missing piece.

In the Beginning

No discussion of influence would be complete without mentioning Dale Carnegie. My introduction to Carnegie came when I was twelve years old, living on a farm in northern Minnesota, attending a school where there were a total of twenty-three kids in my grade. Everyone knew everyone else. Then my parents did the unthinkable. We moved. I transferred to a school of 286 kids when I was in the seventh grade. I now didn't know anyone! My father gave me Carnegie's *How to Win Friends and Influence People*. I devoured that book, studied it from cover to cover, thinking it would make me the most popular girl in school. I thought I would quickly make friends if I just followed the steps. Where could I go wrong if I could make people like me, win them to MY way of thinking, and be liked instantly? I thought life had just gotten better.

My mission became to win these friends and influence them. Well, have you ever tried to influence 286 seventh-graders? Did my determination work? No. But it was my first real exposure to reading about, learning, and understanding human behavior. I was hooked at the early age of twelve.

Here is what I did learn from Dale Carnegie: all of my actions create consequences; it takes effort to understand another person's point of view; and people are creatures of emotion, not logic. Although Carnegie's ideas were (and still are) brilliant, I thought something was missing.

The long-held, traditional methods around influence are that you need to do something or an action has to take place in order to achieve a result. Even though you may not have been aware of the terms for such dynamics, we've been taught early on that influence means you build social proof, instill urgency, promise popularity, or create the illusion that there isn't enough (commonly known as the scarcity principle). What all these methods have in common is that they are based on an external event—and to some extent these methods promote a manipulative or calculating process and are doomed to be short-lived. Under this definition, when you walk into a room, you have to consistently DO something to get people to react or respond in a certain way, preferably the way you want them to act. You have always have to be "on."

Being Influential is the Key

It would be exhausting forcing ourselves to constantly

do, do, do in order to get, get, get. What if you were doing the wrong thing? What if it didn't make a difference? What if what you were doing didn't last?

The good news is that real influence - being influential - can be cultivated, learned, and enhanced. Essentially, becoming influential is a process.

Real influence is not the exclusive property of elite, educated, or exceptional people. Real influence is available in great supply for everyone, once they know where it begins, the true foundation. My clients are relieved to know that there is a better way, a new perspective, and a longer-lasting approach. Anyone can learn to use real influence once they know what it is and where it comes from.

The long-standing beliefs about what influence is and how to do it had me asking some important questions: What needs to happen *before* I start influencing myself, another person or a situation? What does a person need to bring to the table? What makes one influencer better than another influencer?

My answer came in looking at the other side of influence. And that's what I call *being influential.* To be influential, all you need to do is walk into a room. No need to say or do a thing. Mahatma Gandhi, Jesus Christ, Mother Teresa, Aristotle, Moses, Martin Luther King Jr., Pablo Picasso, and William Shakespeare, to name a few, were influential. They are people who had influence even though they did not have a title, money, a position, authority, or power. They shared a message or idea in such a way that attracted people. People were impacted by their confidence and courage in speaking out, in daring to present a new idea, a new perspective, or in offering a better way.

Being influential is a higher order of influence. If you have influence, you will not always be influential. However, if you are influential, then you will always have influence.

Many people confuse, misuse, and substitute these two words. "Influence" and "influential" are different. The connection between "being influential" and "having influence" is this: you have to "BE" a certain way in order to "DO" or to have a major impact on a situation or person.

Having influence results from an external event, whereas being influential results from an internal process. Having influence is about title, authority, money, or position. Being influential is about testimony or your reputation. Having influence occurs as a result of your focus on the other person. Being influential comes from focusing on you first. Influencing is designed to create a change in behavior or beliefs that may not last. Being influential creates a shift in another person where when they experience a conversion, it lasts forever. Thus, having influence is a state of doing, whereas being influential comes from a state of being.

INFLUENCE	INFLUENTIAL
External Event	Internal Process
Title	Testimony
This is About "Them"	This is About "YOU"
Making a Change	Creating a Shift
State of "Doing"	State of "Being"

Here's the litmus test for knowing if you are influencing or being influential. Ask yourself this one question: If I remove my power, title, money, position, or authority, will I still be influential?

If the answer is yes, then you are an influential person.

Being influential is the process of two emotional states coming together, yours and the other person's. You are entering their emotional state, which leads to a powerful connection between two people. Entering another person's emotional state gives you the opportunity to be the best you can be. Connecting on an emotional level is what moves people to action. In order to move another person to action, whether it's to perform better, develop their leadership presence, or make a decision, you need to connect to that person on a deeper level. Real influence happens when you do more than just get them to owe you a favor, or build a sense of loss if they don't do this or that, or act as the expert so they will follow your direction. Real influence is not a power play. You are not "wielding" anything over them.

Real influence is about establishing a connection based on integrity and expressed with authenticity. Real influence is about who you are, the impact you have on others, and how you show up. Real influence starts with being influential.

Who has a longer-lasting impact on you: the confident person who is empowering you to take a risk and share your talents or the person who relies on being your manager, who signs your paycheck, as a way to get you to perform? That's the difference between being influential and simply having influence. If Jack was no longer your manager with the power to pay and promote you, would you still feel his impact? If not, his power is in his position or title, and titles come and go. A person with true influence needs no external title or power. A person who is influential can lead a horse to water and make him drink simply by being who he is. No force, no coercion, no tit-for-tat tactics needed.

Change versus Shift

Setting your stage for being influential means understanding the difference between a state of "doing" versus a state of "being." When you're in a state of doing, you do just that, but successful leaders and influencers have enough to *do!* They know the secret lies in a state of "being" —not just in doing tasks, tips, or tricks designed to persuade, manipulate, or intimidate!

What is the difference between making a change and experiencing a shift? You can change an idea, a habit, your clothes, or the words you use. For example, you can change another person's behavior because you have money, position, or power. But nine out of ten times the person will revert back to their previous behavior and what you "influenced" them to do doesn't last for the long run. To maintain the change in behavior or new belief, it needs to be constantly reinforced. It requires continuous support and bolstering to exist. The thing about making a change is you always have the option to change back. You can choose to revert back to the old habits, outdated ideas, or words that really don't serve your conversations.

But when you experience a shift, you cannot return to what existed before that shift took place. You cannot "unknow" what you now know. One exercise I use to help my executive clients realize the difference between shift and change goes like this. I tell them, "Close your eyes. Imagine walking into a white room, shiny white floor, clean white walls, soft white curtains, and on the right wall there is a closet door. It has a bold brass knob; you reach out, turn the knob, and open the door. Behind the door in this closet, you see an elephant wearing red high-top sneakers! Now you close the door and leave this beautiful room. Open your eyes. Can you forget that you saw an elephant wearing red high-top sneakers behind the door you opened? Will you ever forget? Congratulations! You just experienced a shift!"

What you want to do is not change someone's mind once, but shift their mindset for the long term to align their goals with yours. A shift needs to be created that will result in consistency, even and especially, when you are absent. The difference between change and shift is permanency. A shift is the experience you have of someone, something, or yourself that stays with you forever. You can't forget it and cannot revert back.

The old idea of influence—creating urgency, instilling reciprocity, or exerting expertise—needs constant reinforcement. But being influential— expressing passion with confidence and trustworthiness—needs very little or no reinforcement. (Don't worry; you can cultivate and grow your confidence and trustworthiness. We'll get to that. It's all part of the process and why ALL of us can become more influential, no matter our career or position.)

Why is this so important in our world, our organizations, and our relationships? The answer is simple: When people respond because of *who you are*, then they will 99 percent of the time respond to *what you do*. And it will happen naturally. You don't have to think about it, plan it, strategize it - you let go of doing and just show up in full authenticity. You, being the best version of yourself, is all you ever have to do, in any room, with any crowd. Let go of trying to how learn how to win friends, or be more persuasive or how to "wield" more influence. Put down your "weapons." It's time to engage in a whole new way. It's time to BE INFLUENTIAL.

Chapter One Checklist

- ☐ Having Influence is not "Being Influential."

- ☐ Influence is an external event. Being influential is an internal process.

- ☐ Being influential is a higher order of influence.

- ☐ Influence is the cornerstone of all human interaction.

- ☐ Real influence – being influential – can be cultivated, learned, and enhanced.

- ☐ Being influential is the process of two emotional states coming together: yours and another person's.

- ☐ Change needs constant reinforcement. A shift needs little or no reinforcement.

Deliver What They Need

Deliver What The Organization Needs

Five Non-Negotiable Characteristics:

Hard Working

Collaborative Spirit

Initiative

Attitude

Genuine Transparency

Deliver What They Need

Ask not what your country can do for you – ask what you can do for your country.

- JOHN FITZGERALD KENNEDY

John F. Kennedy's words from his influential 1961 inaugural address can still inspire us to recognize the need and importance of serving others, and reminds us that we all bring something to the table. Let's apply this quote to the organizations and companies we work in. Do you feel that most people only consider what their company has done for them lately? Instead, how different would work life and business be if we asked, "What can I do for my company today?"

I believe in looking for opportunities, sometimes even around corners, but I subscribe more to making my opportunities. This requires asking myself how I can show up better, go the extra mile, ask tougher questions, and hold myself accountable to the job I promised I would do. There's a sense of purpose and pride in knowing that I have the fortitude to give back to the company or organization that employs me (or the client that hires me).

As an employee, there's a sense of responsibility knowing that you make the decision to participate in a community that invests in you; thus in turn, you also invest in them. It's a two-way street. You don't acquire influence simply by working at an influential company. An organization becomes influential because of its people. They know how to hire the right people, and how to develop them. Do you consider yourself someone who is the "right people"?

John Lasseter, former President of Pixar Pictures and current chief creative director of Walt Disney Animation Studios (and *Frozen's* executive producer), was once asked in an interview what he thought was more important: having the right people or having the right ideas. He responded with a laugh saying, "The right people. If I have the right people, I know they will give me the right ideas."

What makes you the right person? How will you deliver what the organization needs? Do you even know what the organization needs from you? Are you ready to meet the needs of your company? Or are you only focused on what you want? In the next chapters we will dive in to organizational needs and personal needs, but you must understand from the get-go that it is a partnership. The organization needs to understand how to help their people and you need to understand that the inherent responsibility to do your best and be your best lies within you.

Every organization, company, or business makes a commitment to their customers, to their brand, and to their employees. They look for people who are willing and able to make and sustain the same (or more) level of commitment to providing more than what was promised. Organizations want people who are dependable, trustworthy, and go beyond expectation.

Successful organizations place great emphasis on prosperity, productivity and profitability. They have to. Organizations need to depend on their employees' willingness to create a partnership to make these goals reality. Employees must recognize the role they play in that partnership. Everything great that organizations produce results first from a partnership that is based on respect and mutually shared values and goals. And things not so great happen when that does not occur.

Case in point. An athletic sportswear company had specific deadlines to deliver their product on time to their biggest distributor. This sense of urgency was relayed to everyone in the company. However, Bob, who had a habit of meandering through his day, wasn't particularly interested in cooperating with this sense of urgency. He had decided a long time ago that he got his work done when he decided it was going to get done. Bob maintained an attitude of *I'm special and the work I do is special therefore people will wait for me to do my job.* Bob's supervisor took a back seat to Bob's attitude, mostly because he was afraid to reprimand or even expect more of Bob than Bob was willing to produce. This unhealthy dynamic went on long enough that Bob felt fairly secure in continuing how he performed.

Because of the company's refusal to address Bob's attitude, they missed deadlines and eventually lost their best distributor. They turned a blind eye to Bob's unwillingness to get on board with the values and goals of the company. Bob wasn't willing to participate in a partnership with the company to make it more prosperous, productive, and profitable. Neither were acting influential and also, simply put, Bob wasn't the right person.

Throughout my coaching career, I have found that there are five non-negotiable characteristics that the right people possess, bringing the right ideas to their organization. These are characteristics that employees, and employees only, can bring to their work. Organizations cannot *"train"* these characteristics into their people.

Five Non-Negotiable Characteristics Organizations Look For

Characteristic #1: Hard working = smart working

At the top of the hard working list is dependability. People who take ownership of all aspects of their job are the people who not only have a clear vision of what is expected, but look further to see what more needs to be done or could be done.

Characteristic #2: Collaborative spirit = dare to share

No person can achieve "greatness" in an organization completely alone. Rather, the right person knows how to share – share their ideas, questions, failures, fears, excitement, frustration, and knowledge. They know how to listen, not only with their ears and eyes, but with their heart. They pay attention to what is not being said and how it reinforces or disturbs the overall company goal.

Characteristic #3: Initiative = always dreaming

People need to create their own self-motivation. A person with inner drive, versus someone who needs constant pushing and pulling, is someone who takes initiative. They are the dreamers of the organization who are always thinking of new and better ways to do, be, believe, think, feel, and act. They are the fire in the belly of the organization.

Characteristic #4: Attitude = failure breeds success

Organizations want people who rise to the occasion, not only getting the job done, but doing it in the face of roadblocks, confusion, and conflict. A never-give-up attitude is what fuels the right person to get the job done in spite of upset, shifting priorities, and changing schedules. An attitude of promoting high morale and team spirit is an essential piece to organizational success.

Characteristic #5: Authenticity = Genuine transparency

Everyone is passionate about something. People who truly believe in an idea and focus on sharing that passion tend to inspire and motivate others to possibility and potential. Authentic people focus on what they believe in whether it's finding sustainable business practices or exploring ways to transport food into the poorest nations. When you focus on what you're passionate about, you'll get people listening . . . and thinking.

These five characteristics are shared by people who are influential. They bring their best game to the organization. Influential people invite their hard work, collaborative spirit, initiative, attitude, and authenticity to be their calling card. These are the qualities that push them over the finish line when it comes to partnering with their organization in order to achieve greatness. Organizations look for and expect to find these characteristics when hiring a partner they can invest in, train, and grow within the company.

John Lasseter often shares the profound insight he learned as a young animator at Pixar meeting his new boss Steve Jobs for the first time. Jobs had one suggestion—"Make it great." The project Lasseter was working on, *Tin Toy*, went on to win the first Academy Award ever given for computer animation and set the foundation for what later would become *Toy Story*. Those words, "Make it great," had lasting impact on Lasseter and he states Jobs' guidance has influenced every frame of every movie he's made since that meeting.

Organizations are looking for people who make it great.

How can YOU show up and make it great every single day? By understanding that is up to you and by optimizing the seven influence traits (confidence, commitment, courage, passion, empowering, trustworthiness, and likeability). Increase your ability to be influential and you become a lasting legacy.

Do Organizations Have Needs and Expectations?

When it comes to being influential, the organization itself is one side of the coin. Real influence depends on what the company provides and what the employee brings to the job. Hence, the reason it is called a partnership.

Companies need people who have imagination and who are prepared to go the extra mile. Organizations want people they can invest in, who make the most of the training and opportunities provided to them. Company culture is crucial to influence and culture is co-created by the organization and the employees.

Business management theorist, Peter Drucker, is attributed with the phrase "culture eats strategy for breakfast." His thinking was spot-on. Organizations provide employee-centric culture and employees produce customer-centric focus. Company culture that gives employees the freedom and opportunity to experiment, shape their work, and disrupt an outdated status quo set the stage for innovative and leading-edge thinking and action. Employees can be amazing once they have permission to go outside the box, looking for better, new, and lasting. Think iPads, *Toy Story,* Spandex, or whatever has inspired you.

While organizations set the "culture tone," employees are expected to bring their best game to the park. Along with opportunity comes responsibility. When an employee walks through the door of an organization, they should be prepared to meet the needs of the organization by showing up as confident, passionate, trustworthy, as a leader, communicator, and team member. Organizations want people to not only bring their mind to work, but their heart and soul. It's the ultimate win-win. People who bring high expectations of themselves and others are more apt to get involved and participate at a higher level, and enjoy their jobs so much more.

Lou Gerstner, former CEO at IBM, once said, "I came to see in my time at IBM that culture isn't just one aspect of the game; it is the game." He knew that organizations have a major responsibility to open the door for people to share and be their best. The IBM turnaround was based on a very simple principle of change – acknowledge the shared values, beliefs, and assumptions people have about where they work. These are the elements that cultivate organizational effectiveness and success.

As we saw with the company who let Bob do his own thing, an organization can either relish in the rewards of employee behavior or succumb to the consequences. It is always best when a problem is addressed head on. Organizations can develop their leaders to be empowered to do so, and when they train their employees in the traits of influence, they find that such problems occur less frequently and with less intensity.

There are primary, secondary, and even tertiary effects on an organization from not addressing a problem or allowing it to linger. Ignored problems have a tendency to cause fallout in four distinct areas for people throughout the company; non-emotional impact (missed deadlines), emotional impact (frustration), cultural impact (lack of trust), and financial impact (lost revenue). Let's take a look at a few examples of the impact problems have in an organization.

Example #1: Take the case of a "slacker" like Bob or many others like him. His work is delayed, the boss is not happy, other people have to cover for him which makes them not happy. Frustration, lack of motivation, resentment abound. The culture becomes one of a lack of trust and people stop supporting each other. This all affects the bottom line of course as deliverables are delayed or not met. Team abilities are wasted.

Slackers at work are a drain on everyone and you can feel the trickle effect of the fallout every slacker leaves in their path. They come in all shapes and sizes. Slackers are the people who check their Facebook constantly, take 2-hour lunches, and are always late on deadlines, IF they meet them at all. Slackers not only refuse to pull their weight, they heap it on someone else, usually the nearest person in the company.

But before you judge the slacker, look closer to see the context of their behavior. Are there troubles at home? Is there an undisclosed health issue? Have they gone through a traumatic life event? All hope is not lost. The solution to suffering a slacker is to motivate them. That's the job of the leader, knowing how to motivate their employees, and that's where being influential becomes so important.

Knowing how to re-engage the employee and build up their trust in their own abilities increases morale and productivity, not just for the slacker but for all around. When projects get back on track and deadlines are met, people sense the commitment to fairness and a supportive workplace returns. Staff will trust the company's ability to solve a problem and will be open to listening and supporting future projects.

People are usually very forgiving if they see effort, if they see the company is confronting an issue, and if they can be part of the solution. This is the underlying impact or influence that dealing with an issue has on the entire workforce.

Example #2: Many organizations face the problem of the micromanager. One of the side effects of the micromanager is that they ruin great ideas, and run promising talent and potential out of the company.

Employees who are constantly criticized may try harder for a while, but they eventually stop trying at all. Decisions are delayed because of only one decision maker, direct reports stop creating and innovating, and people do not feel valued or appreciated.

When working with a micromanager, there is a loss of mutual respect and trust. Fear-based decisions occur and silos are created. Valuable ideas are never heard. The company can show a loss of profit, loss of market share, and/or a loss of standing or position in the industry.

But take a look at what happens when you empower people. They take ownership, which means they assume accountability. People who are empowered sense a feeling of trust from their manager. They dare to make it great. It's the person who dared that discovered penicillin, post-it notes, the engine, and electricity. The list goes on and on. When you give people the freedom to succeed and fail they will do both. And the wise manager realizes that failure is often times the key to success.

When an organization knows how to create an empowering manager, employees take responsibility and assume ownership of the process which in turns means they will make better decisions and engage in a higher degree of collaboration. Employees feel a sense of pride and purpose in their work when their contributions are valued. People have fun and get excited about work again - and will forgive company mistakes.

The financial effect is an increase in employee productivity and accountability. Costs are reduced. People are on fire to outperform the competition and innovate the next best thing. Employees take seriously the well-being of the company and enjoy the flexible and engaging work culture.

When you hire the right people and create the right influential atmosphere, employees go the extra mile for the company. They brag about working for the organization. They take pride in getting the job done and doing it right and seek ideas and actions that support even greater achievement. It's an upward spiral.

Example #3: Any organizational problem or issue can be addressed through the eyes of developing influence. For example, think about lack of engagement. People are not talking to each other. Perhaps they have nothing to say, which if that's the case, means they're not doing their job. Territories and borders are drawn up. Then the competition begins. People compete for resources and recognition. They see the enemy within their own company walls.

However, when engagement is encouraged and rewarded trust builds. Ideas are shared. People feel secure. People find a new and fresh commitment to the mission of the organization. The impact of instilling engagement and interaction at all levels and across all functions in the company is enormous. Does higher retention and less turnover sound appealing? How about increased employee satisfaction AND customer satisfaction? That's the outcome of developing true influence.

Example #4: When strong influential leadership is lacking, everyone and everything pays the price. Poor decisions are made and tolerated. Fear skyrockets because people sense they are on the wrong path or are pawns in a game called business. Lack of strong leadership relies on smoke and mirrors. Ineffective leaders are like moving targets, i.e., once you get close enough to understand or ask questions, the target moves once again. It creates chaos and havoc.

Whereas, when a company is led by strong influential leaders, a culture of integrity is born. People are inspired and hopeful. They are no longer afraid to challenge the status quo. They believe in relationships and connection because that is what feels right to them. They realize strong relationships are the defining factors of successful organizations.

Everyone in an organization is a leader no matter their position. People first learn to lead themselves, then the team, then the company. They lead ideas, processes, and opportunities. Once an organization creates influential leaders and an influence culture, they experience great benefits:

- Increases trust and respect of employees
- Creates buy-in
- Establishes relationship and connection
- Ability to lead in the face of fear or uncertainty
- Inspires people to become better and achieve the "impossible"
- Builds empathy and understanding
- Promotes vision and values
- Solidifies a culture of integrity
- Reduces careless behavior/decisions
- Increases reliability and dependability
- Increases profitability, productivity
- And many more!

One thing all of the above problems have in common is the severe blow they cause to the bottom line. An organization that builds an influential culture creates happy satisfied employees that will always go the extra mile. And that means more profit.

Chapter Two Checklist

- ☐ Success is a partnership between organizations and employees.

- ☐ Don't stop at just finding opportunities. Make your own opportunities.

- ☐ Companies want people who have imagination.

- ☐ Employees can be amazing when they bring their best self to work.

- ☐ Culture isn't an aspect of the game – it is the game.

- ☐ No person can achieve "greatness" in an organization completely alone.

- ☐ When you show up fully, you get your needs met.

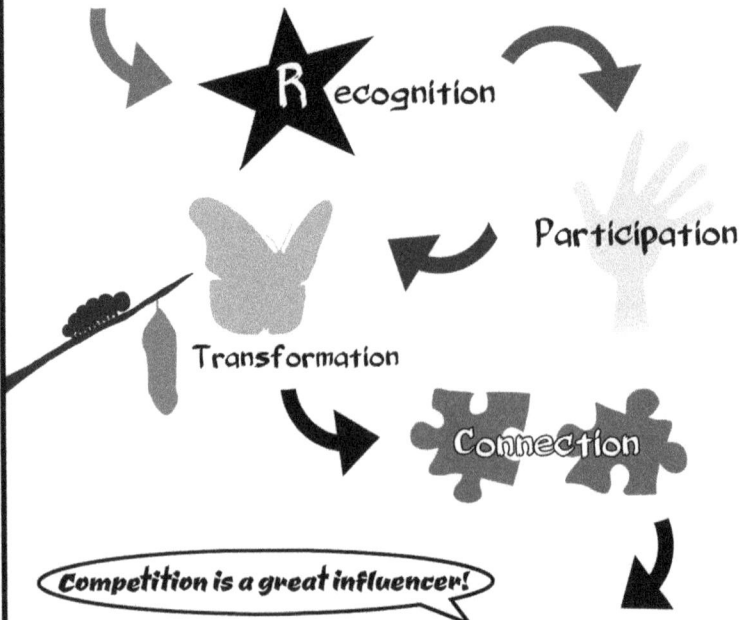

CHAPTER THREE

Organizational Culture and High ROI

The organization is, above all, social.
It is people.

- PETER DRUCKER

B
eing influential is something you can't see or touch. However, it is the most valuable commodity possessed by an organization.

To become truly influential, the organization must pay close attention and deeply listen to what they hear and observe. They commit to provide the culture where people within that culture or community can exercise their responsibility to meet their organizational needs. Every person and team within an organization of any kind has organizational needs - needs that can only be met together with the organization. Influential leaders *understand* and open the door for those needs to be met.

Having a clear understanding of and responding to those needs keeps the organization moving forward toward shared and desired goals. This creates a sense of ownership and accomplishment throughout the organization and strengthens employees' connection to the organization. When people are connected and aligned with the organization that is when good things happen.

Learning what people need depends on trust. People have to know that they won't be yelled at, criticized, dismissed, or ridiculed for speaking up, for being transparent about their needs. It is important for the leader to institute a trusting organizational climate where people are more likely to express what is on their minds. And this is where the organization will access new information and knowledge – from its own people – their most valuable asset.

However, recognizing the needs of individuals and teams isn't just for the leader to do. This can come from anyone in the organization who has the opportunity to observe or hear what is going on. What are people missing? What are they complaining about? What do people need to do their work? Everyone is a stakeholder when it comes to the organizational needs of its people. This is truly the cornerstone of stakeholder-centric organizations.

An influential organization is one where the people are committed to the company's vision and how they will make that happen. People courageously share their passion knowing it can inspire creativity and innovation. They place great value on mutual trust and respect. And they empower themselves and others to stretch beyond the impossible. The influential organization has defined a new level of engagement and a better way to achieve success. They garner a more profound loyalty and motivation from the people they call family.

Why do the most influential organizations create a culture where individuals and teams can *meet* their needs?

Because they realize that in order to stay on top of their market, and have a healthy, prosperous bottom line, they need to do more than hand out a paycheck. They know it's about loyalty, commitment and respect. When employees' needs are met at this level, they know that the company they work for is interested in them as people, not as a means to an end.

We all know that plants flourish when they get water and sun. They grow strong. Their flowers are fuller, more colorful and their buds are abundant. The same thing happens inside the influential organization. When people receive the attention, connection, and knowledge that they are valued, the return on that type of investment is priceless.

Four Common Organizational Needs That Must Be Met to BE INFLUENTIAL

There are four common organizational needs (of people and teams): recognition, participation, transformation, and connection.

1. Recognition

People don't just want to be want to be recognized and valued for the work they do – they need it. And they should not have to ask for recognition. For instance, when an organization fails to acknowledge a person's never-give-up attitude or refrains from giving timely feedback on progress, the person may become despondent and downhearted. For example, Sarah is a diligent worker day-in and day-out coming up with solutions and always a cheerleader for the whole team, yet her efforts and attitude go without recognition. Sarah thus begins to question her own sense of self-worth to the organization and the meaning of the work she does. Eventually, she feels constantly overlooked and feels she is not important.

Recognizing the person who puts in long hours, meets deadlines, imagines the best ideas, and collaborates well with others (to name a few) gives the organization a leg up on its competition. Providing well-deserved recognition retains the best employees while at the same time attracts the highest talent. Acknowledging a person's hard work or great idea instills confidence in their work and spurs greater ideas. Recognition is so simple and yet often does not occur.

For instance, Linda was an ER nurse in a 175-bed hospital that was widely recognized for providing top quality service to the community. This hospital consistently won awards and received high grades in all healthcare delivery standards. Linda took a great deal of pride in being part of the team. She had the habit of coming in early and leaving only when the job was done. She cared about the patients and she loved what she did.

However, the hospital wasn't invested in sharing feedback about Linda's dependable performance. It was rare for her to hear how and if she was truly valued for what she did. Over the years, she just accepted that it was her job to treat sickness and unexpected tragedies. Linda feared that she would appear to be big-headed to expect any sort of gratitude for her work. She certainly wasn't prideful, but there always was a nagging hint of "Would anyone notice if I were gone?" Linda had been at this hospital for more than sixteen years. She couldn't remember the last time anyone pointed out something she did that made a difference to the team, the hospital, or a patient.

This organization didn't understand human nature. They appeared to be stuck in the old mantra that if you compliment employees they'll lose their drive to achieve and excel. It didn't occur to them that Linda (and others) were not feeling appreciated or valued. By not cultivating the emotional climate of the hospital, they were alienating people and creating an environment of something less than it could be.

This behavior, or lack of behavior, is all too common. To start on the path to being influential, an organization needs to ask a few questions. How should we acknowledge our best, most loyal employees? Every employee? How can we make the recognition personalized? Is it unexpected? Is it specific? How can we foster a place where loyalty and motivation transpire? Imagine how different Linda's view of herself and the hospital would be if her organization understood just a little bit more about human needs, and acted on it.

2. Participation

People need to participate in a culture of a collaborative community while maintaining difference. In other words, people need to not be criticized for their competitive and unique nature. Being competitive and collaborative can co-exist in the same environment.

Jonah Berger, professor of marketing at the Wharton

School in Pennsylvania states, "Having a competitor slightly ahead of you is a huge influencer." He points out that basketball teams who trail badly at halftime most often lose, but teams that are down by only one point at halftime tend to come back and win. What this means is that when we place ourselves in competitive environments where there are co-workers or outside brands slightly ahead of us, we tend to push the envelope to seek to overtake them. We access our courage and make a stronger commitment to win the race.

People are made better by the positive influence others can have on them. This often comes in the form of competing for the gold. The very act of being challenged means you are competing at the very least with yourself. It is what is unique or different about each individual that allows them to successfully compete at that level. People need to participate in a collaborative way where they have freedom and autonomy to take on new challenges that stretch them.

In the early months of her employment at a medical research institute, Tanya was part of a team that was responsible for researching the effects of certain pharmaceuticals on the liver. Tanya graduated summa cum laude with special honors in a Ph.D. biochemistry program. She excelled in her courses and research, outshining most other students. Tanya obviously had specialized skills and talents that gave her a strong competitive edge in her work.

The research company she worked for recognized Tanya's abilities immediately. They understood that Tanya had a strong need to compete, to find the answer or resolve the problem. In this case, Tanya's nature was a valued trait; to be a quick thinker, possess critical problem solving skills, and be ambitious. Not wanting to discourage her ambition and curious nature, they placed Tanya on a team of outstanding and accomplished scientists.

This organization understood that the uniqueness that made Tanya stand out among her peers would be a prized asset to this team. She thrived in a collaborative environment that challenged, respected and fostered her unique abilities. They were not afraid of her competitive nature, because they understood that was the fuel that made her who she was. It was also the inspiration that led to great scientific results. Tanya had great passion for her work, and she was allowed the freedom to exercise that passion to its fullest.

Tanya was afforded the opportunity to do what she did best. All the while being surrounded by people who had a positive influence on her. Instead of trying to dissuade or stifle Tanya, the institute understood that when competitive minds are able to collaborate, innovative results will emerge. That was a smart (and influential) organization. They knew how to meet Tanya's organizational needs.

3. Transformation

The third most common organizational need people have is experiencing transformation at work. This sounds heavy, but it's really not.

The most powerful contributor to success in any positive, structured change is honoring who you are "being" in the experience, not just focusing on "doing" the activities that are expected. This involves having an awareness that inspires us to embrace the deep meaning of our core values. This is the foundation for the biggest shifts to occur. That's easier said than done, but you can't skip this step and expect sustainable growth.

Transformation is a difficult concept for a few reasons. First, the future state (what we are transforming to) is unknown, and is found through trial and error. This isn't something that can be managed on a timeline. Quite the opposite. The actual change process emerges as you go. Second, what awaits us in the future (when the transformation has occurred) is so profoundly different than the present state that new mindsets and behaviors are essential. It requires an inner shift of our perspective and culture.

How can an organization satisfy a person's need to experience transformation?

By inviting them to get involved in the new vision, the new process, or even their own challenges. What we do know is that employee resistance is in direct proportion to the degree to which people are kept in the dark and out of the transformation process. Successful transformation means mistakes. People will make mistakes. There will be failures. There will be confusion and chaos. But there will also be discovery, opportunity, and innovation. Before people can really make a contribution, they need to accept they are not perfect and will fall down in the process. The influential organization knows this and provides the necessary support, coaching, and investment.

Even though Tom was superior in his performance and output, he begin to question if he was making a difference on a grander scale. After all, he never saw the results of his work. Tom believed something was missing but he couldn't quite put his finger on it. He was doing the same thing every day. Could that be it? He started realizing he didn't have the same passion he once did for his work. In fact, he started feeling like a robot, doing the same thing day in and day out.

Tom needed something new, something that would challenge his mind, his spirit. He wasn't satisfied. He wanted to experience something different but wasn't sure what it could be. Tom confided in his supervisor, Jackson, that he felt empty about his work. He shared, "I feel at a loss. I'm not sure what is wrong or if anything is wrong."

Jackson consoled him by saying, "Oh, Tom, it will pass. I've had those days and I got over it."

What Jackson didn't hear was Tom's cry for help, his need for transformation. Tom was counting on his supervisor to offer more than a "you'll get over it" nod. He needed guidance to figure out what was going on. Unfortunately, Jackson was ill-prepared to coach Tom. He did not recognize that fulfillment and challenge was missing for Tom. Jackson was not confident in just listening to Tom. He wasn't sure how to empower Tom to work through his discontentment. Jackson didn't know how to work through his own discontentment and didn't have the courage himself to reach out.

This is typical in organizations. People at all levels are not equipped to recognize the intangible or covert things that are happening with their peers or direct reports. Because they are not prepared, they stumble, brush it under the rug, hoping it was just a fleeting occurrence. When this happens what could have been a positive growing experience (transformation) turns into a disturbing problem. In this case, Tom moves on to a company that invests in his growth and values him as a person and meets his organizational needs. That is the difference that an influential organization understands. They also train their managers to reach their own influence potential.

4. Connection

Lastly, people need to foster strong relationships at work. It's important to know there are people at work who care about you beyond the fact that you are the only one who can navigate the monster database system to maintain compliance with regulatory and policy requirements. People have a strong basic human need for connection and camaraderie especially with a group of people where they spend more than half of their waking hours. (More than a third of our entire lifetime is spent with our coworkers!)

According to the Gallup Organization, people who have a best friend at work are seven times more likely to be engaged in their jobs. And it doesn't have to be a best friend. Gallup found that people who simply had a good friend in the workplace are more likely to be satisfied.

This is a very good reason to encourage positive relationships between and among the employees in your organization. People are naturally social creatures. We crave positive interactions. Good relationships give people freedom to focus on opportunities.

Trust is the foundation of every good relationship. When people trust their boss, their team, their co-workers, they develop a powerful bond that leads to better communication. Trusting and being trustworthy lead to transparency and honesty in your thoughts and action. This removes the energy-sucking practice of having to "watch your back."

What happens when a company doesn't foster positive work relationships and connections?

Just ask Morgan. Morgan is the marketing coordinator for a large manufacturing company. He left a previous position where he had a good salary, people who respected him, and an environment that supported his strategies. He was very creative and his marketing efforts paid off both with customers and the company bottom line. Morgan left because he wanted a change and the perks and opportunities for advancement were better at the new job.

After several months, Morgan realized he made a mistake. His immediate boss, Peter, a senior executive, had no desire or interest in Morgan's development. Peter was rarely available for conversations, reviews or overall quality time with Morgan. Rather he was more interested in keeping Morgan, in Morgan's words, "dancing." Morgan was required to keep Peter informed of every detail of every action he took. He spent way too much time doing these reports than his actual job. Morgan approached Peter, asking to meet on a regular basis to talk about growth or about new perspectives on marketing methodologies. Didn't happen. Instead, Morgan received sarcastic remarks in front of colleagues, or worse yet, he'd be inappropriately challenged.

The tension became so obvious that it affected how others related to Morgan. Because of the power of the senior executive Peter, team members tended to avoid Morgan for fear of being seen associating with him as being supportive. It was obvious to Morgan that his boss, Peter, would feel threatened if he believed Morgan was developing good relationships with others.

The relationship between Morgan and Peter was miserable. Peter only focused on faults with no emphasis on strengths. Morgan had no idea when he'd be blamed or contradicted. It was like walking on eggshells. Least of all, Morgan's talents and initiatives were not appreciated. There appeared to be no chance for Morgan to develop any resemblance of a positive relationship with his boss.

It would seem that Peter was fairly insecure. He lacked the confidence or courage to nurture and support a relationship with Morgan. Peter didn't know much about empowering others to be their best or make mistakes along the way. Sadly, Morgan experienced his boss to be untrustworthy and not likeable – traits that often are taken for granted in forming quality relationships. Morgan missed the connection and respect he felt at his former organization and realized that a larger paycheck was not worth the trade-off.

Every human has these organizational needs (recognition, participation, transformation, and connection) and an influential organization and leader understands that cultivating the groundwork in meeting those needs is crucial. When an organization places a focus on relationship satisfaction in the workplace, happy, healthy, fulfilled employees are more productive than those who are not. They take fewer sick days and have a higher degree of engagement throughout all levels and across all functions of the company, both with people and processes. Research shows that engaged employees are more likely to go above and beyond their job responsibilities, roles, and duties to do more than is expected. They will assist peers or colleagues in accomplishing their work, and they will look for opportunities to drive innovation. That means a better bottom line and everyone is happier.

Organizations are leading the change.

Times are changing. Many organizations are changing the way they approach people development and performance management. Companies now treat performance development as an ongoing process rather than a once a year event usually conducted via a performance appraisal. Although product and service is of utmost importance, today's influential organizations realize the significance of people and purpose in achieving great products and service. They are no longer putting the cart before the horse. In fact, organizations are placing greater emphasis on development – developing the influence of their people.

Organizations who meet the work needs of their employees are influential organizations. When they see and understand the simple picture of what makes employees happy, it leads to better performance. People are most happy at work when they can be passionate about what they do. When they can make a commitment that supports their core values. When they are trusted. And when they can empower colleagues to step up.

People follow people they can believe in, who they trust to help them achieve their goals and meet their organizational needs. They have an innate desire to be inspired, respected, and heard. They need to know they make a difference and have the opportunity to improve.

They need to feel supported in developing their skills and they need to believe they can be more than they were yesterday.

There's the story of an old country farmer who was taking his nephew camping for the first time. His nephew had five degrees – was one of the smartest men alive. They set up their tent and quickly fell asleep. In the middle of the night the farmer woke up his nephew and said, "Look up, what do you see?" The nephew said, "I see millions of stars." The farmer said, "I know that but what does it tell you?" The nephew said, "Astronomically, it tells me that there are billions of galaxies. Meteorologically, it tells me it's going to be a beautiful day. Theologically, it tells me God is a great creator. What does it tell you?" The old farmer shook his head and said, "It tells me somebody stole our tent."

Sometimes a person's organizational needs are obvious (the tent was stolen), but not seen very clearly. An organization is often overwhelmed with responding to the customer. Measuring up for the competition. Making the grade for the shareholders. Learning ever-changing technology. In light of all of this, the influential organization believes in understanding and meeting the organizational needs of its employees. They put employees first.

Like I said in the beginning, this is about going back to basics. This is human nature and common sense. With most things, simple does not always mean easy, but at least now you can comprehend that becoming influential does not have to be complicated. It simply has to be made priority number one. Becoming influential is a game-changer.

Chapter Three Checklist

- ☐ Learning what people need depends on trust.

- ☐ Everyone is a stakeholder when people's needs are met.

- ☐ Influential organizations build culture where people and teams can meet their needs.

- ☐ Four Organizational (Work) Needs People Have
    a. Recognition
    b. Participation
    c. Transformation
    d. Connection

- ☐ Organizations need to understand human behavior.

- ☐ Collaboration can only exist when differences are present.

- ☐ Competition is a great influencer.

Essentials YOU Bring to the Organization

Meeting Personal Needs Improves Performance

Six Basic Human Needs:

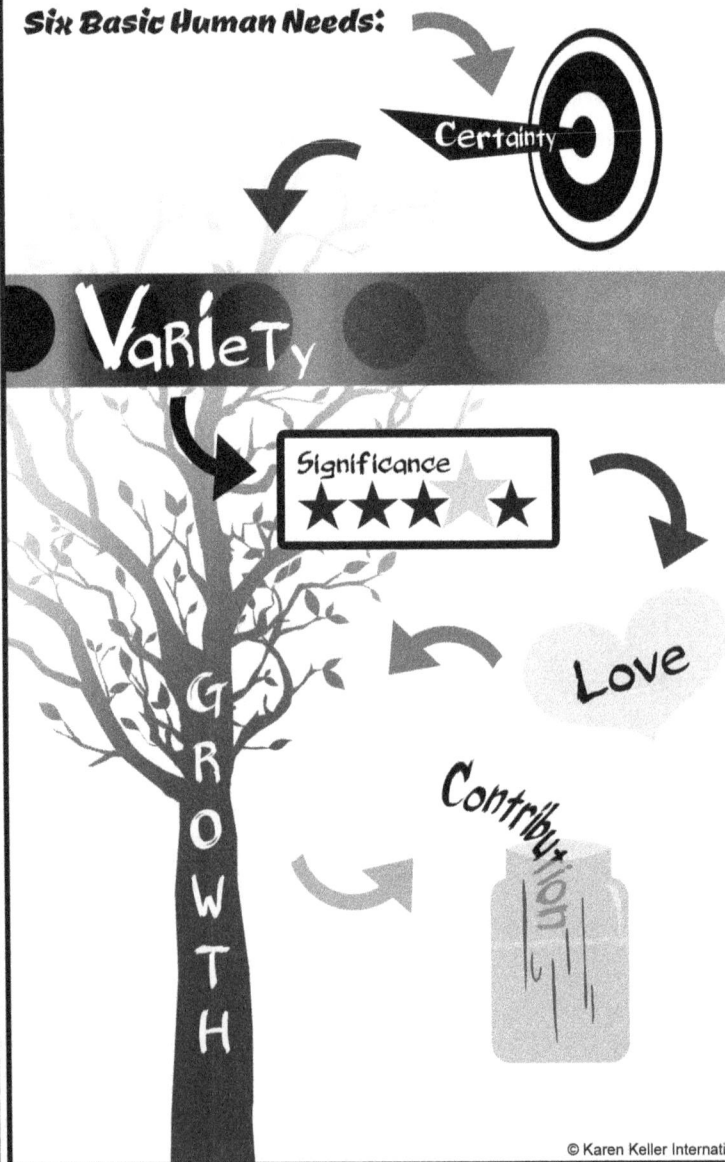

Certainty

Variety

Significance
★★★ ★

Love

Growth

Contribution

Essentials YOU Bring to the Organization

Who shall set a limit to the influence of a human being?

- RALPH WALDO EMERSON

Influential people are likeable, trustworthy and courageous. It's their presence, their confidence, their passion, or their ability to empower greatness from those around them that makes the influential person able to get their message across to create a behavior in you or interrupt or stop your decisions or actions.

They have the ability to commit to something greater than themselves. Influential people are able to face their fear while living their passion. The way they achieve this level of living is by knowing and fulfilling their own personal needs. There's a reason the airline attendant instructs us to put on our own oxygen masks first. You have to honor and respect yourself to know that your own needs are crucial for you to serve others in any capacity at all.

You've heard it said countless times that you cannot help anyone until you first take care of yourself. Those with real influence walk their talk. They understand that they have to model what to expect in others. You cannot operate with a "do as I say, not do as I do" mentality. Think of a father who tells his teenage son not to drink and yet he comes home drunk every Friday night. What is influencing his son, his words or his actions? If your boss harps about timeliness and deadlines and yet shows up late and goes home early, what kind of influence is happening there? How a person lives their life, at work and at home, day in and day out, is the power of influence. Being influential means you are congruent. Your actions are in alignment with your words. You are a credible role model.

Being influential means you realize that you have needs that must be met in order to be your best self, in your personal and professional life. And you can't look to anyone else to make sure your personal needs are met. No matter how great (or not), your organization is, the buck stops with you.

Personal Responsibility

It is your personal responsibility to take care of your own personal needs. Yes, to retain valuable talent, an organization has to meet the organizational needs of their people, but organizations can only do so much when it comes to personal needs of employees.

We, the people, have an obligation to bring our best to our work. That starts with becoming aware of our own needs, not only as a worker, but as a person.

When a person is able to identify and meet their own

personal needs, life takes on a new meaning. It is then we are capable of experiencing the passion that is at the core of our existence. If you had to choose between living a life with passion or a dull humdrum existence, what would you choose? Exactly. We know that it is possible to enjoy life more fully. To get to that point, we need to understand the six personal needs and how to satisfy them.

Six Personal Needs Common to Everyone

Human Needs Psychology (Maslow 1943) identifies six emotional and psychological needs of human beings (which have been re-introduced popularly into the public arena by self-help guru Anthony Robbins): certainty, uncertainty/variety, significance, love and connection, growth, and contribution. We constantly work daily to satisfy these needs on a subconscious level. These six human needs are not wants or desires; they are needs and they motivate our every action and decision.

1. The Need for Certainty

You have the need to feel safe and to have some semblance of control and protection in your life. Our brain is designed to predict what will happen next. It does this so we don't experience the pain or displeasure of "not knowing" what is happening next. Human beings detest the unknown. In fact, that is what we worry about most.

Jeff Hawkins, Executive Director and Chairman at the Redwood Neuroscience Institute explains the brain's preference for prediction, "Your brain receives patterns from the outside world, stores them as memories, and makes predications by combining what it has seen before and what is happening now. Prediction is … the primary function of the neo-cortex, and the foundation of intelligence."

Not satisfying our need for certainty can have damaging results. For instance, John was a commodity manager at an international aircraft company that was acquired by a larger equipment maker. John heard the rumors of a big takeover, plummeting profits, and major changes lurking around every corner. John wasn't shy about asking for information and seeking to understand what was going on. He was concerned about how the new acquisition was going to affect his position and his future at the company. Weeks went by where John heard nothing. To make it worse, John and others were told that things would be "fine" and to "not worry." They were given empty promises of "things won't change." John was frustrated and worried about his career, his future, and his family. Because the new company fell short of providing sound information, acknowledging people's fears, and failed to provide future direction, John left. And with him he took the knowledge and experience of a 15-year employee dedicated to the company.

2. The Need for Variety

As much as we crave predictability and need to have order and control, we also like to mix things up from time to time. With the need for variety, you are striving for a little (or a lot of) uncertainty in your life in order to relieve boredom, predictability and stagnation. We all have the desire to live an interesting life where there may be some challenges, excitement, and fun. We want to know that dinner is usually at six but we also like to break free of rigidity from time to time. They say variety is the spice of life and we don't want meat and potatoes every night. Humans toggle between the need for certainty and the need for variety. People who have an extremely strong need for uncertainty can be classified as dare devils, like Evil Knievel or Harry Houdini, but all of us like to change things up sometimes. A new shirt, a new lipstick, trying a new place to eat.

Paul's decision to invite a little variety into his life was spurred by a desire to connect better with his teenage children. Paul's idea of what constitutes "real" music is of course drastically different than that of his kids. One day Paul decided to go out on a limb and listen, really listen, to his children's music. Although he found it difficult to entertain at first, he went from song to song. He eventually began to appreciate the styles, rhythms, and message that came from this music. He actually enjoyed something new and different. Paul's first reason to do this was his need to connect better to his children, but it also met another need – the need for variety, newness and change. We all know how we like to discover new things to keep life interesting. We want (and need) this on the job as well.

3. The Need for Significance

The need for significance is the need for a feeling of importance or worthiness. Your objective is to create a sense of identity. This need also appeals to our competitive nature. Professional athletes have a strong need to excel by achieving something greater than other athletes in their sport. Their need for significance is strong. We all have varying levels of this need, but all humans need to feel significant in their personal and professional lives.

Stan Smith, one of the greatest tennis players in the world, was once rejected from being a ball boy for a Davis Cup tennis match because event organizers felt he was too clumsy and uncoordinated. Smith went on to prove them wrong, showcasing his not-so-clumsy skills by winning Wimbledon, U. S. Open and eight Davis Cups. His talent and drive were fueled by his need for significance, not just his natural athletic ability.

4. The Need for Love and Connection

The need for unconditional love is probably our strongest need. Striving to connect and have strong social bonds is why we get married, participate in religious activities, gather at parties, and why some people join gangs. It's all to fulfill the need to be connected to other people. That includes the workplace.

The Gallup Organization identified that one of the key pieces to retention of talented employees is they have a significant emotional connection to at least one person at work. Having a best friend at work, someone who cares about them, who values who they are, is indicative of the highly productive workplace.

Lisa, the medical manager of a large surgical group, was involved in all the day-to-day decisions as well as the long range planning. Lisa formed valued authentic relationships with people at work, in particular with the managing partner, Dr. Vickie, a surgeon who respected the knowledge and innovative ideas Lisa brought to the practice. Dr. Vickie honestly cared about Lisa. She respected her intentions for growing the practice. Beyond feeling recognized for her hard work, Lisa knew Dr. Vickie cared about her. She trusted her and believed that Dr. Vickie would be helpful in times of stress and challenge.

Because Lisa had a good connection, she looked forward to her job, had a high commitment to quality, and worked hard to build engagement and interaction among the rest of the staff. Being regarded for who she was paved the way for Lisa to perform beyond expectation.

5. The Need for Growth

The need for growth means that you strive to learn, experience and grow mentally, emotionally and spiritually in a variety of ways throughout your life. Growing means satisfying your curiosity, your desire to explore, or expanding your mind. When you stop growing, a sense of lack or dissatisfaction starts to develop. If you are not growing, then you are not making any real progress in your life.

Carlos couldn't get up early enough to start on his latest venture. He was determined to keep working on his tech project until he had a breakthrough. Carlos' need to expand his mind and grow was so great he was virtually unstoppable. There wasn't much of anything that he wouldn't tackle to prove to himself that he could learn it. Carlos was a solid musician, good cook and a respectable collector of comic books, but his main interest was the world of technology. The idea of escalating the potential of his latest project was the most exciting thing for him. Carlos loved learning – and having fun in the process. His need for growth kept him feeling alive.

6. The Need for Contribution

The need for contribution means you strive to contribute to something greater than yourself. You have a strong desire to add value to other people's lives – a value that goes beyond meeting your own needs or wants.

The servant leader is in a position to make a difference by believing in and promoting the best people have to offer. This leader enriches the lives of individuals, builds better organizations creating better business and a better world. Doing meaningful work is where people have the opportunity to contribute beyond their own desires. When an organization creates buy-in from its employees to a meaningful mission or purpose, people then rise above the occasion to contribute. They know their work has significance impacting the lives of others.

One thing that marks every long standing organization or institution is the ability of the leader to transfer purpose, vision and meaning to the next generation, so they can continue to influence and to carry on the legacy. One such leader was Martin Luther King, Jr.

King acted from the realization that something needed to change, equality should be for all people. This realization tapped into his need to contribute to a cause that would have wide-standing effects for millions of people. Not knowing the figure he would become in history, he accepted the opportunity to make a difference in any way he could. He did this by being influential, courageously and passionately leading a cause greater than himself.

Meeting Your Needs

When your personal needs are met at a high level, you experience great satisfaction and fulfillment in life. It makes you feel good to be alive. On the other hand, when your personal needs are not satisfied, you end up feeling a sense of loss, distraction, and stagnation. Satisfying or not satisfying these basic human needs will reflect in the decisions you make, the opportunities you take advantage of, and the quality of your relationships.

Think of the artist who molds the clay. Even though the clay is the least expensive element of the pottery process, it is actually the most important. Having the right clay opens up new areas of creative exploration. But if the clay is dry, absorption resistant, or too rough, it will have a negative impact on the finished product.

Just like the potter who chooses the right clay, it is your responsibility to offer your best to the organization and you do this by first satisfying your personal human needs. Remember, you need to put on your own oxygen mask first. You must take care of you; it is no one else's responsibility.

Now that you've learned or relearned these basic human needs, it is up to you how you prioritize them. You need to identify if your current behavior, choices and decisions are aligned with how you prioritize your needs. For example, which need do you value more than another need? Are your current decisions and choices in conflict with how you would like to prioritize your needs? Are you experiencing contribution or growth in your life? What has to happen to support a balance between each of your personal needs and the way you want to live your life?

Meeting your personal or basic human needs motivates your behavior. Achieving your full potential (self-actualization) depends on meeting these needs, which in turn predicts your ability to reach peak performance in your career, in your job, and in your community. Human motivation is based on people seeking fulfillment and change through personal growth.

People who are meeting their personal needs focus on what is going right, rather than what is wrong. For example, Abraham Lincoln, the 16th President of the United States, rose above losing his mother at age nine, surviving two business failures, losing in eight elections, burying two sons, and living with severe depression. In spite of everything President Lincoln lived through, he was fully engaged with learning (growth), experimented with new ideas to solve problems (variety), acted on strong ethical/moral standards (certainty), formulated a sense of identity even in the wake of popular opposition (significance), connected to the heartache of people on both sides of the Civil War (connection), and underwriting a cause greater than himself (contribution).

Impact of Personal Needs on Organizational Success

There is an old saying that you are three people: the person you believe you are, the person others think you are, and the person you really are. When someone becomes too much of what others think they should be (overcompensation for the need for connection), it can disrupt their ability to contribute in ways that come most naturally to them. When this happens, it becomes difficult for the person to grow, innovate, and find opportunity. Not meeting your own personal needs carries over into the workplace where you can feel misrepresented, misjudged and underutilized. Everyone, regardless of hierarchy or rank in a company, is subject to this dynamic.

If you are not satisfying your personal needs, finding satisfaction in the workplace will be difficult and challenging at best. This is when your job becomes a duty or obligation to fill - a means to an end. Passion is missing, commitment wanes. You feel stuck and confused. Your skills are not developed. Your identity has become what others expect it to be. This impedes your ability to successfully meet your personal and organizational needs. When your sense of identity is lost, you become a replaceable commodity, rather than a valued asset.

Influential organizations are wise to provide a workplace environment where people can express their authentic identities by way of meeting their personal human needs. However, it is up to the employee to do the work of being themselves, not hiding from others, or falling into the trap of being whom everyone else expects them to be. You risk not being efficient, productive, or making a difference. Ultimately you won't be content which impacts your happiness which impacts the company bottom line.

The importance of personal needs cannot be stressed enough. You are responsible for meeting your basic human needs. But be real. It is unrealistic to expect that you will find love and connection with everyone you meet. That's okay. Knowing that someone at work cares about you is enough.

In order to successfully meet your basic human needs,

you need to believe in yourself (confidence), make a promise (commitment), take the risk (courage), and access your purpose (passion) to take the steps to open the doors to connection, to having significance, and to experiencing uncertainty.

Give yourself permission (empower) to explore ways to achieve degrees of your personal needs. Just as you would encourage a child to walk, you need to extend that same encouragement to yourself. Trust yourself.

Taking care of your own personal needs does not happen overnight. It takes time, effort, and commitment. Realizing that it's up to you is the first step. Elie Wiesel, Nobel Laureate and Holocaust survivor, said, "Ultimately, the only power to which man should aspire is that which he exercises over himself." That is how you begin to tune in to your influential self.

Chapter Four Checklist

- ☐ Influential people have an influential presence.

- ☐ Influential people have the ability to commit to something greater than themselves.

- ☐ Six Basic Human Needs
  a. Certainty
  b. Uncertainty (Variety)
  c. Significance
  d. Love and connection
  e. Growth
  f. Contribution

- ☐ Retention of talented people begins with an emotional connection.

- ☐ Deliver your best to yourself first.

- ☐ Meeting personal needs motivates positive behavior.

- ☐ Becoming your influential self begins with taking charge of you.

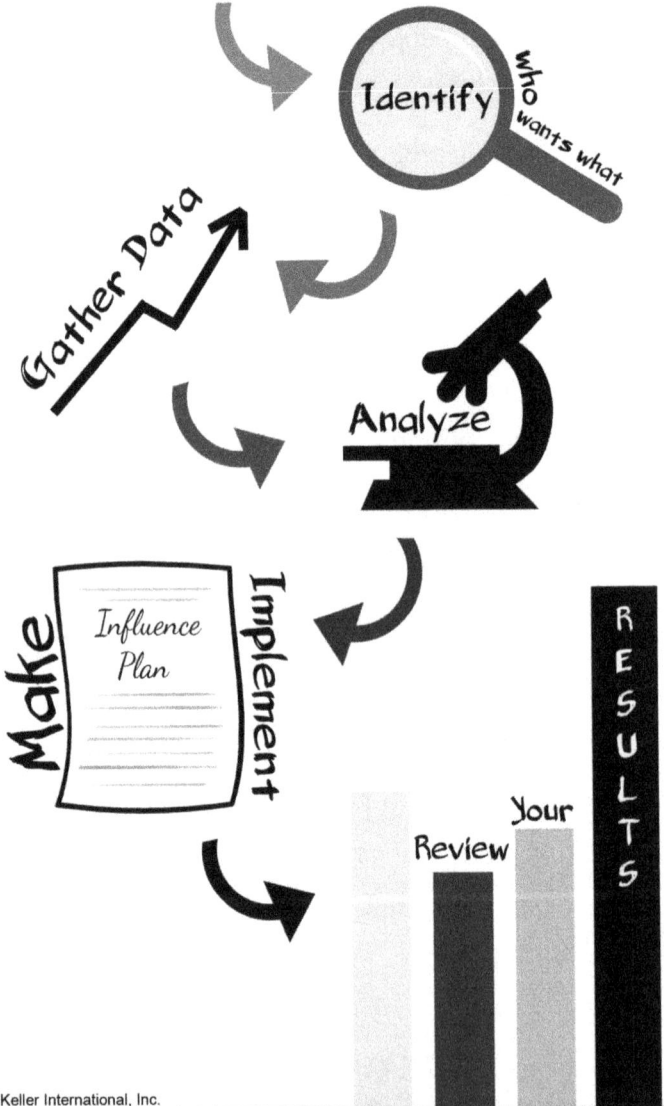

CHAPTER FIVE

The Company & Employee Partnership

At the end of the day, you bet on people, not on strategies.

- LARRY BOSSIDY
Former CEO, AlliedSignal (Honeywell)

W
e live in a world of irony. Many organizations worry about the minute details of running the company, but remain blind to the needs of the people who are responsible for those details. Eventually this leads to the expansive practice of paying attention only to what is urgent over what is really important.

Former U.S. President Dwight D. Eisenhower, quoting a former college professor, said in a 1954 speech: "I have two kinds of problems: the urgent and the important. The urgent are not important, and the important are never urgent." This "Eisenhower Principle" is said to be how he organized his workload and priorities. When you look at your organization, does it seem that all the "urgent" to-do's just aren't that important in the grand scheme? It can be easy to get off track and that is why being influential matters so much - it helps you see the big picture and the details, and also what is truly important.

Organizations have the obligation and opportunity to organize and prioritize the value of the company, the human capital – all employees from the CEO to the doorman and every person in between. The most effective way to grow human capital is to first accept that human capital is the true worth of a company, and next, protect it at all costs.

The Council of Institutional Investors controls approximately three trillion dollars' worth of securities and assets. During an interview they were asked what they look at to determine the worth or value of a company. Their answer: the people in the company. The Council stated that a company's value lies between each employee's ears. And, when employees leave a company, they take their value with them.

Meeting the *organizational needs* of employees is critical in defining identity and satisfaction as contributing human beings. Meeting *personal needs* is not up to the organization yet important for every individual to be aware of as efforts to satisfy these needs drives our thoughts, feelings and behaviors. The question then becomes, "How do we connect these two groups of needs?"

It's critical to align a person's organizational needs and personal needs. Why? Finding and *keeping* the talent. Every organization is constantly on the lookout for the emerging leader, the best strategist, most skilled, most gifted, or the High Potential. They are looking for TALENT. More specifically, hidden talent.

Influential Organizations Discover Hidden Talent

Why is it so important to cultivate people's commitment, courage, confidence, etc.? Because once you do, you will discover a wealth of hidden talent. Why is it so important to discover the hidden talents of the people in your organization? In nature, eagles can fly between 75 and 125 miles a day. Wild elephants can roam up to 50 miles a day. If that eagle or elephant is locked-up in a cage, they're not living the way they were made to live. They've been stifled, suffocated, trapped. And the same thing can happen to people in your organization. They are not fully expressing who they are and what they are capable of doing. They are not exercising their full influence potential and thus neither is the organization.

Uncovering unique talents indicates why one makes certain choices, enjoys certain activities and is better at some things than others. Discovering what people are particularly good at or competent at can take time to figure out. Once you identify those hidden talents, embrace them and use them in creating an influential culture. When confidence or commitment or trustworthiness or likeability is missing, talent tends to go underground or goes missing altogether. Talent is there but it does not shine or peak. To bring forth the hidden talent, the organization needs to develop these crucial traits in their employees. Organizational success depends on it.

Organizational Needs + Personal Needs = Highest Performing Individual

In order for these two sets of needs to align, the organization needs to provide the environment where an employee can reach their full potential as an employee. This goes beyond merely providing an accurate job description. Although it is important that the organization defines a person's purpose in the organization, how feedback is given, and the expectations they have, it is the wise and influential organization that pays attention to their employees' needs for recognition, participation, transformation, and connection.

Just as the organization has responsibility in this alignment of needs, so too, does the individual. An employee needs to take ownership over how their personal needs are met in all areas of their life, including their work life. They are responsible for establishing meaningful connections, certainty, significance, variety, growth, and contribution. It is up to the individual to meet their needs in order to offer their best to the organization. The alignment and connection of satisfying organizational and personal needs is a partnership between the organization and employee.

Aligning Your Organizational Needs With Your Personal Needs

To build a trusting and loyal partnership, there are specific steps in the alignment process. First, you need to **identify who wants what.** What does the organization want from the individual? More risk taking? Better communication? Increased trustworthiness? And what does the employee want from the organization? More support? Better opportunities? Consistent feedback?

Whatever both parties want or need should be at the forefront of the discussion. If there's any uncertainty about what is wanted then further discovery needs to take place from both sides.

Second, **gather the data.** Find out what is missing for the employee and what's missing for the organization. What are the facts behind certain decisions? Who is responsible for what? How will disagreement be handled? How will each participate? How will the person meet the organization's expectations?

Gathering data also includes finding out what assumptions are being made. Do people assume you don't care? Are there impressions that need to be cleared up? Look for the unspoken rules that exist.

Third, **do an analysis.** Look for new perspectives on what this partnership will look like – or should look like. Talk about the benefits to both parties of meeting these needs. How will you align the organizational and personal needs with the goals and objectives of the organization?

Adrienne was a highly experienced executive with specialized skills in finance. She built an extraordinary resume showcasing her achievements, projects, and international success. Adrienne was used to being courted by high-caliber companies. An international financier consulting agency caught her attention. Upon the first meeting, she was surprised by their very different approach compared to past experiences with other companies.

What she noticed was the company started the

negotiation process by stating where they placed their attention in bringing people on board. They said they realize the importance of the needs of all employees from the top to the bottom. Everyone was afforded that same consideration and opportunity. This company believed that people are happiest when they can go to work where they can solve problems, make things better, grow with each other, and make a difference. They shared with Adrienne that they can teach people their jobs, but by investing in how they get their needs met is when the whole company thrives. Adrienne was dumbfounded and very pleased. They were influential in winning her over. She now holds a senior position with this finance company.

The fourth step in building a partnership between the organization and employee is to **make an Influence Plan.** Begin to strategize what you need to do to build alignment between your organizational and personal goals. Once you identify the specific actions or behaviors that need to occur, the changes you need to make, the effort you need to expend, the resources you need to uncover, the opportunities you need to explore, then ask yourself this question, "What will it take for me to carry out this plan?" Visualize the possibilities. Clearly define what needs to be done.

For example, while creating a plan to satisfy his organizational need of participation, John, a middle manager in the operations department of a large auto supplier, wanted to have greater input into the department's decisions. Part of his plan was to ask his supervisor how he can participate more in team meetings and be included in the decisions of the department. To go even deeper, John began looking at how his confidence would help him articulate what he had to offer the team and the department. He started considering how to build the courage he needed to have the conversation with his supervisor. John was also aware of the value of being trusted so that people would listen and value his ideas and concerns.

In short, John was looking beyond the short-term aspects of his plan. He wanted to work on what would give him the greatest chance of this being successful. He explored what he could do that would assure success of his plan, i.e., his confidence, courage and trustworthiness. That is where John began his work.

The fifth step in aligning your organizational and personal needs is to **implement your plan.** You need to put it all into action. As you discover what needs to be enhanced or maximized, be it your confidence, your likeability, or your passion, you have to practice. Practice having difficult conversations. Practice staying calm so you can better listen. Practice engaging people. If growing your commitment is needed for you to take steps to get into a position that matches better with your skills, then do it. Incorporate into your plan how you will improve your ability to make a commitment.

You cannot treat symptoms without understanding the cause. To have lasting impact with your plan, you need to tackle the foundation of what is really causing lack of action, bad habits, reservations, or unproductive behavior.

The sixth and final step is **review your results.** It doesn't do much good to have success and not understand how you got there. And likewise, it doesn't do any good to meet with failure and not understand what you needed to do differently or what you learned. Find out what needs to change, what you missed in carrying out your plan, or how well prepared you were to succeed.

Personal Needs at Work

Personal needs can be met everywhere in your life, at home, with family and friends, at work, in the community and with a peer group. Personal needs are always with you. They aren't something you deposit at the door when you walk in to your office or the plant floor. So how does a person acknowledge their personal needs at work?

The personal need for certainty corresponds well with the organizational need of participation and a personal need of connection. As human beings, it is important that we can have some control over what we do at work by getting involved and working alongside other people, as well as experiencing a connection with others who share a similar desire.

For example, Matt was frustrated that people didn't acknowledge him. He wasn't taken seriously, mainly because he had a fun good nature about him. Matt felt misunderstood to the point of losing a sense of belonging. He mustered up the courage to tell his boss exactly how he felt and the effect it was having on him. Matt's boss, Art, had no idea what was going on with Matt. In fact, Art was slightly perplexed because he thought Matt was happy.

There were several dynamics that occurred in this scenario. First, Art didn't pay attention to Matt on a level that required real listening. He didn't take the time to have a conversation with Matt to actually find out if he wanted to take charge or have input into decisions that affected him. Second, because Art was basically oblivious to Matt, it caused Matt to become increasingly irritated. He was dissatisfied and exasperated at trying to understand why people didn't pay attention. Third, Matt and Art both made assumptions that were entirely false. Matt wasn't happy and Art wasn't dismissing Matt. Fourth, Matt learned through coaching that there were things he could take control of and put into action. Once Matt worked on building his confidence and courage, he was able to approach Art. He shared how he felt and what he needed to be happy at work. Art was flabbergasted. He had no idea. But once he did, he apologized for not taking the time to notice or ask what was going on with Matt. Together they put into place a plan where Matt would get his needs for participation and connection met. Can you guess the result this had on Matt's performance?

When the organization and the employee work together and share the responsibility to meet the person's needs, the benefits are obvious. The organization becomes a healthier, more positive place to work, which inspires trust and stimulates a collaborative and cooperative work environment. Just as you look for the underlying reasons that cause problems, you can also look for underlying reasons that lead to an influential culture.

Another illustration of bringing organizational and personal needs together is the organizational need for transformation and the personal need of significance.

Clint had just completed his Master's Degree in biochemistry with a health and medical concentration. As you might guess, Clint had intellectual horsepower. He also had a strong desire to make a difference (personal need of significance) for the greater good. During many interviews while job searching, Clint encountered the attitude that the most important thing was the bottom line. Although Clint was aware of the need to make money to keep a company going, he also wanted more. He then interviewed with a company who made chemicals and cleaning supplies for commercial grade use with operations all over the world. Something that particularly interested Clint was their operation in Africa. There was a real need to help countries there purchase and use soap, but it was difficult for a variety of reasons. Clint accepted a position with this company on the condition that he would work in their African offices. Clint had so much passion that he had an idea and over a short period of time he developed a soap that the people in these countries could make and use without causing any environmental concerns. Not only was Clint a genius, the need to make a difference (personal need for significance) where he could have a major impact of something greater than himself (personal need for contribution) fit in with his organizational need for transformation. Are you seeing how this works?

The bottom line is that the work a person does in the organization has to be meaningful in their personal life. The worst thing an organization can do is ignore or dismiss the organizational needs of its employees, and employees need to stop putting their personal needs aside. Meeting these needs leads to personal satisfaction that is brought into the workplace.

Meeting your personal and organizational needs has a direct impact on how you respond to others, how well you connect, and the health of your relationships. The obvious impact is more engagement, better decisions, and increased performance at work. But there's a greater impact. And that is the effect that meeting these needs has on your life, every experience, and every relationship.

Chapter Five Checklist

- ☐ Importance should never suffer at the hands of urgency.

- ☐ Influence belongs to all, from the Chairman of the Board to the person answering the phone.

- ☐ A company's real value lies between each employee's ears.

- ☐ Hidden talent exists everywhere in every organization at all times.

- ☐ Meeting organizational needs AND personal needs produces a high-performing individual.

- ☐ Being influential is a partnership between the organization and the employee.

- ☐ Work has to be meaningful to an individual's personal life.

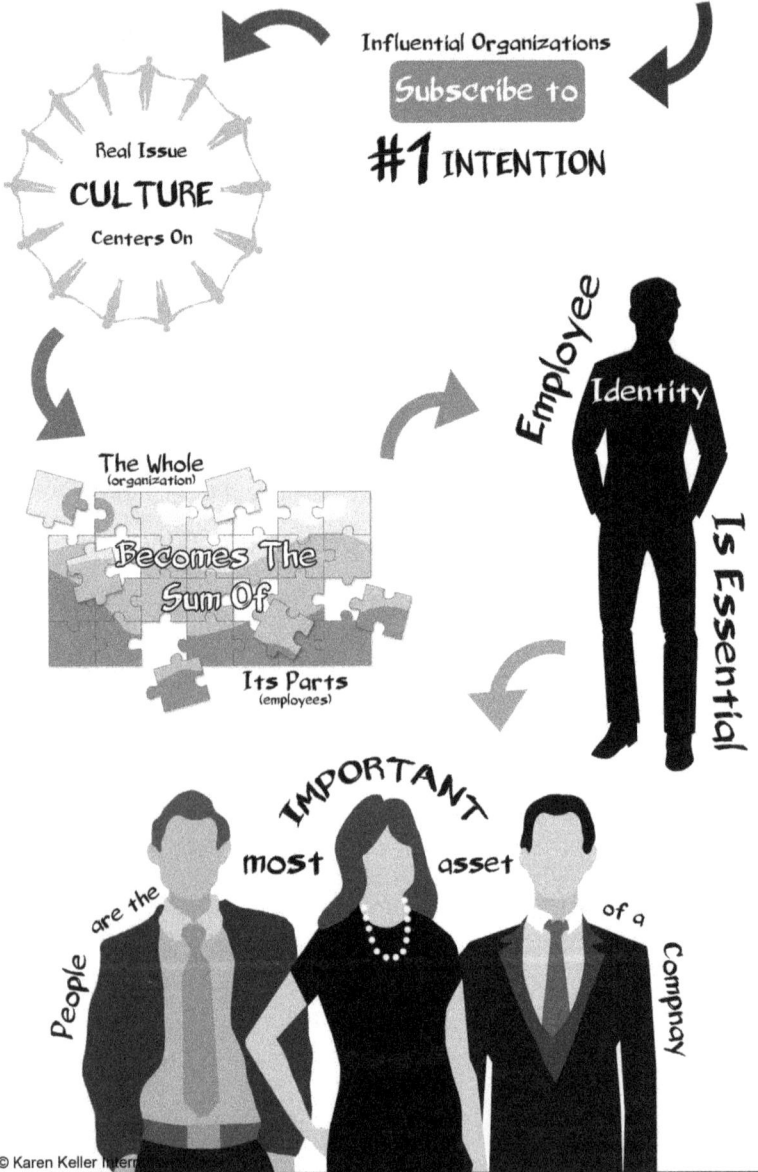

CHAPTER 6

Employee Identity and Teams

The Team With The Best Players Wins

Influential Organizations
Subscribe to
#1 INTENTION

Real Issue
CULTURE
Centers On

Employee
Identity
Is Essential

The Whole
(organization)

Becomes The
Sum Of

Its Parts
(employees)

IMPORTANT
People are the most asset of a Company

© Karen Keller Inter

Employee Identity and Teams

The team with the best players wins.

- JACK WELCH

The person you are at home is the person you are at work. If not, you are wearing a mask on one of those stages, and that does not bode well for influence. Being influential starts with how we influence ourselves. It takes a lot of confidence and passion to say no when we have to, or say yes when we want to. It takes a great deal of trust to go looking for an opportunity and if that opportunity doesn't exist, to create it.

Every organization has the opportunity to create a space where people can get their personal and organizational needs met. If the opportunity is not there, you as employee must create that opportunity. Every person in an organization should adopt the entrepreneurial mindset of seeing beyond the obvious, taking risks, and seeking the unknown.

Organizations need to allow people to influence

each other, to impact each other in a positive way, a way which might shake up the company. It might disrupt the culture, but that's part of the risk to getting to something that's greater than what already exists. Being able to acknowledge both your personal and your organizational needs, and then to achieve them takes a lot of influence, first on yourself, then on others around you. An influential culture allows everyone to thrive.

Ask some common sense questions. How are we working alongside each other, respecting each other's positions, but also each other's needs? How are we responding to people? When we know that Jane or Jack has this particular need, how do we respond to that? How do we help or encourage a co-worker to meet that need? Is that something we are capable of doing? If we're not, we need to say we can't meet that need. There's too much "stuff" going on in our organizations where people don't want to speak up. It's like the little boy who spoke up about the emperor's new clothes, or lack thereof. People are afraid to really tell the truth, but that can change.

Alignment of Personal Core Values and Organizational Goals

Where do core values fit into this equation? Do core values even matter? Is this something an organization should pay attention to? Should an employee place importance on their core values at work?

Accepting that human capital is the most valuable asset of a company requires decision makers, owners, or boards to recognize that human capital goes far beyond the actual work output. Because business is about people, the true value of the company goes right to the core of every person in that company – their core values. Being influential depends greatly on how your core values align with the organization's mission, goals, and expectations. Core values provide guidance in decision making, problem solving, and finding ways to exploring opportunities. Core values guide our decisions, predict our behaviors, and determine the depth of our loyalty. Core values need to be the essence of how you live your life and there is nothing that will cause you to violate that sacred commitment.

For example, Susan was asked to position information in such a way that would make the company third quarter look better than it was in reality. One of Susan's highest core values was honesty and truth. She instantly felt a lump in her gut, because she understood the company was expecting her to innocently look the other way. But she couldn't. Susan wouldn't violate her long-standing commitment to her core value of honesty. Instead, she told her boss that doing this would be stressful for her, and that she couldn't. She knew she would be risking her job. But her core value, honesty, was more important to her than her job. It was a core value because there wasn't anything that would cause her to violate it, even losing her job.

Every influential organization reads the pulse of their employee's core values. They work diligently to hire the right people, nurture innovative ideas, and create the best fit between a person and a position. It means developing people from a new perspective, where the person is seen through the lens of who they bring to the work they do.

The #1 Thing Influential Organizations and People Subscribe To

INTENTION.

Influential people know intention is the driving force for developing purpose and meaning. Intention sets the course for action. A person without intention is a person without purpose, wandering aimlessly trying to be influential, without their actions being connected to their core values and beliefs. Intention flows without burden when it is in line with a person's core values and beliefs.

Influential people set intentions that give them a framework for the priorities they set, and how they align themselves with the resources they need to use to reach their goals.

Meaning is the secret ingredient for being influential. Influential people understand that as their self-awareness expands so does their capacity for understanding the meaning behind their actions and thoughts. If we're too invested in protecting ourselves, we fail to reach that deep level of understanding and meaning. Protecting ourselves, or believing we need to protect ourselves, begins to upset or undermine our true intentions. We either question our intention or we challenge it, all because we have not realized the meaning of our actions.

To illustrate this, an executive I coached, Jeff, had the best intentions to do everything he could to make his team successful. He provided the necessary resources, spent many hours listening to new ideas, counseled (and forgave) people their mistakes, and went the extra mile in encouraging learning at every turn. One day Jeff realized that one of the people on the team was undermining his efforts. Ordinarily, he would have confronted or brought this awareness to the person who was doing the undermining. However, that person was the company owner's nephew. Jeff had to consider consequences not only for the team, but for himself as well. Jeff had a choice to make - risk fallout from the owner or work quietly hoping things will change, i.e. protect himself. This wasn't an easy decision.

Jeff did take the risk. He brought it to the attention of the nephew, giving him the opportunity to make the necessary changes in his behavior. Unfortunately, the nephew didn't respond well. Jeff then approached the boss, sharing everything that was happening. The result? The boss supported him and dealt appropriately with his nephew. The boss even went further and assured Jeff that he needn't fear dealing openly and honestly with problems, even if it meant stepping on a few toes.

Although Jeff had a difficult decision to make, he stayed true to his core values and to the meaning behind his efforts of developing this team. He knew that growing this team was instrumental to many facets of the company. He wasn't inclined to ignore that. In his mind, Jeff made the only decision that he could. But what stands out is this: Jeff was a confident committed man who went the extra mile. He was passionate about his work. Jeff empowered others to bring their best to the job. This is what the boss knew and respected about Jeff. It was who Jeff was as a person that he understood what Jeff had to do.

How Essential is Employee Identity?

Which would you admire most, the richest company in the world or the best place to work in the world? Simple. The best place to work in the world. I would also bet it's the richest company, too. Why? Because when you provide a culture where people can express themselves, contribute their best, and engage fully, you get a company that delivers. It doesn't matter what, they simply deliver.

Because we have become very global in industry, commerce and trade, and impact, defining company identity is important. We hear about brand and reputation but where does all this truly originate? The people. It starts first with the people's identity. How does a company build the identity of their people? They start by looking at how they impact each other. That's what brand is really all about. It's how we are impacted by what we see on the shelf. The color, the words, the way it makes us feel. And the culture of what happens inside our organizations is no different. The only difference is that most people don't KNOW how they impact others. They are clueless. And beyond that they don't understand why they have the impact they do, once they discover the impact they have.

One of the reasons people don't pay attention to their identity is because it is not valued. If knowing how you impacted others was important (which it is), then companies would plan and spend the resources to help their people develop from this avenue. Once a person's identity is developed and they stay true to it, it will drive growth. Identity needs to be pared down, to the foundational pieces, to what people can take ownership over, which a company cannot control. Then the company needs to translate what people develop into everyday practices by making their goal developing people's capabilities.

Every employee needs a personal brand, the culmination of who you are, what is unique about you, your signature image. You are not a talking head. You are a person who has unique talents. Your brand needs to support your company's mission. It starts with self-awareness. It begins with one voice – your voice. Culminating into many voices.

Mark wasn't accustomed to speaking up even when he had lots to say. His tendency was to listen to what other people said, observe what the most popular view was, and then take a side. What Mark didn't realize was this was how he stifled his own passion. He didn't ask the important questions leading to finding his purpose. His voice is the underlying why of his passion. Finding his why would clarify many things going forward and prevent personal (and organizational) drift, where Mark would gradually forget his own ideas, thoughts, and opinions. Mark risked losing his personal focus. Mark was working with an executive coach who pointed out these observations. The coach questioned Mark on the future consequences if he continued to stifle his voice. Mark was totally unaware that he had reached this point. It happened so gradually that he didn't even notice.

Mark began to face the conflicts he was living by not speaking up. The more his awareness grew, the more his courage grew. Mark developed the courage to explore his why. Why he felt the way he did, why his ideas could be innovative, why he could make a difference in outcome, and why he could provide teachable moments.

Steve Jobs was a Why fanatic. Jobs' personality

sometimes rubbed people the wrong way at Apple, but through it all, the Apple people understand the method behind his madness. Steve Jobs recognized the power of the Why, instilling it in all facets of the company with the hopes of Apple remaining a leading innovator even in his absence. I hope the map Jobs left for the next generation of Apple leaders will lead to influencing a greater future.

What is the Real Issue?

The real issues for today's executives and managers center on people and culture. How do we attract world-class talent? How do we develop them? How can we build a culture that allows the organization's talent to embrace new risks and opportunities, a culture that works together to see the possibilities arising from change and not as a threat? If we can create this environment, an organization will be agile and ready to adjust to the world of today and tomorrow, and we will enjoy it. It starts by being stakeholder centric. This is an often misunderstood concept. It has nothing to do with money, but it does have to with how every person from the bottom to the top is invested in the success of the organization. That is the secret sauce of an influential organization.

The Importance of Organizational and Personal Needs and Teams

Individuals on influential teams connect their goals to the goals of the team. They desire to learn and look at all points of view offered from other team members. They place great importance on how relationships effect change.

Influential organizations expect their teams to align their actions and decisions with the strategic plan, value diversity of thought and ideas, and manage conflict to lead to new solutions, not letting it destroy progress.

Because we are social by nature, when we congregate in groups or teams at work, our personal needs are front and center. This is natural. Our teams become more effective and inspiring when the team members achieve their needs from the work they do on the team.

How is meeting your personal and organizational needs beneficial to a team?

Ken Blanchard said, "None of us is as smart as all of us." When the organization meets the collective needs of the people on a team the team thrives.

People want to be in a collective environment with groups and teams where they can realize their sense of purpose, knowing they are making a difference. People are eager to differentiate but they also have a strong need to bond. We are funny creatures that way. Influential teams result from building a foundation of cohesiveness and understanding that is born out of developing the uniqueness of each team member.

Let's take a look at the six human (personal) needs and how they play out in our groups and teams in the organization.

Certainty and Teams

The main ingredient of stardom is the rest of the team.

- JOHN WOODEN

Meeting the need for certainty means helping team members find the best stimulating balance of certainty by keeping them informed and providing clarity about the project they are trying to achieve, and what is expected of them. When we are not able to meet our need for certainty, we get stressed, which leads to being over-controlling or expecting others to be perfect.

The way to help team members achieve their need for certainty is to keep them in the loop. Share information, direction, and most importantly, changes to goals or methods to achieve those goals. It's also important to let people know how they fit into the larger picture. To completely succeed at meeting this need, you develop and nurture your passion and commitment.

Variety and Teams

Uncertainty is a very good thing: it's the beginning of an investigation, and the investigation should never end.

- TIM CROUCH

Oddly, just as we crave certainty, we need variety (uncertainty), change, something different to keep life exciting and interesting. Having new experiences helps us feel energized and involved. When a team member seems to initiate conflict or confusion it might mean they are bored and want to shake things up. They need the entertainment this provides, although it's damaging to the team.

Providing different activities or a range of tasks satisfies the need for variety. The team can take on new goals, a change in how they achieve those goals, or new team members that offer a new skill set and perspective.

Significance and Teams

Success is when I add value to myself.
Significance is when I add value to
others.

- JOHN MAXWELL

People thrive when they are active in something meaningful. They want to know that what they have to offer is important. Influential teams let their team members know they are valued and needed. Team members are more motivated and take ownership for the work they contribute to the team.

To nurture significance, the team needs to acknowledge a person's work, taking the time to recognize what they are learning or the role they play in the team. It is human nature and common sense that everyone responds to "nice job."

Love and Connection and Teams

We need 4 hugs a day for survival.
We need 8 hugs a day for maintenance.
We need 12 hugs a day for growth.

- VIRGINIA SATIR

It should go without saying that we need to connect to others, sometimes people who are similar to us and sometimes to people who are drastically different from us (variety – these needs pop up everywhere!). We like to feel close to people on the team, to know there's a special bond whether it's because we are working on the same project or because we've become friends.

Connection comes from setting up a team environment where individuality and community can co-exist. Connection results from sameness but also from difference. I am interested in people who have different experiences than me. Connection happens when the team members respect and learn about each other's strengths and challenges. This brings a camaraderie to the team.

Growth and Teams

And what, Socrates, is the food of the
soul? Surely, I said, knowledge is the
food of the soul.
- PLATO

We all have needs to learn and grow. Unfortunately, sometimes those needs get sidelined once we become adults. Even so, our curiosity still lives inside us and drives our need to explore and find out what's on the other side of the door.

When you can make learning and growth a top aspiration among your team is when innovation and creativity surge. When people know they have the freedom to question the status quo, think outside the box, or disagree as a way to move past barriers, the team becomes ultra-productive. Expect them to test their understanding of what they believe. Challenge your team to go deeper.

Contribution and Teams

Research shows that the climate of an organization influences an individual's contribution far more than the individual himself.

- W. EDWARDS DEMING

Our need for contribution refers to contributing to something greater than ourselves, for example, being part of the team who is on the hunt for the cure to cancer or heart disease, or being on the engineering team that is exploring space travel. You know your work has huge manifestations beyond what is happening from day to day.

Help the team see the association between what they are doing and the value it adds to a greater cause. Make sure they can see the big picture and the important role they play in bringing it all together.

Provide Opportunities

To benefit from building an influential team, the organization has to take the time to find out which of these needs is most important to each team member. Notice and ask questions about what motivates each team member to take action. Discover what inspires them to stay in the race or not give up. Find out what it is that makes them dig a little deeper or stretch themselves to achieve.

Providing opportunities for people to meet their organizational and personal needs builds alignment between their core values and the organization's mission and goals. When this happens it creates a healthy and influential organization. If this is missing, it's similar to what would happen if middle C was missing on a piano. Just imagine how different or ineffective the sound would be. The chords? The music? Imagine how different Tchaikovsky's *1812 Overture* would sound? Or the Beatles' *Let It Be?* You could say that middle C is the most influential key on the piano, the basic central key that everything starts from. How influence itself has been viewed for all these years was missing the essential key, just like middle C, and that key is that influence is not an action, but a way of being. The whole missing piece to influence is that we didn't understand it all begins and flows forth from first being influential. An individual and an organization can now tap into their potential for influence and learn how to build on it.

When organizations make available the resources for people to develop their confidence, trustworthiness, courage, and likeability that is when the organization is perceived as confident, trustworthy, courageous and likeable. The whole (organization) becomes the best sum of its parts (employees). That is what it means to be influential.

And it can be learned.

Chapter Six Checklist

- ☐ Effective influential teams know how they fit into the bigger picture.

- ☐ EVERYONE responds to "nice job."

- ☐ Individuality and community can co-exist.

- ☐ The best teams are challenged to go deeper.

- ☐ Influence is not an action, it is a way of being.

- ☐ The whole (organization) becomes the sum of its parts (employees).

- ☐ Curiosity should always live in each person.

CHAPTER 7

The Seven Influence Traits®

Never Underestimate The Importance Of The Basics

ACTION IN

LIKEABILITY

CONFIDENCE in Motion

TRUSTWORTHINESS By DESIGN

YOU

power of COMMITMENT

Living With

PASSION

COURAGE into INSIGHTS

EMPOWERING with purpose

You Are The BEST Asset You Will Ever Have

© Karen Keller International, Inc.

CHAPTER SEVEN

The Seven Influence Traits®

Never underestimate the importance of the basics.

- TOM PETERS
Author, In Search Of Excellence

A person's attention span today is reportedly only nine seconds. Thus you don't really have time to DO anything to influence another person, however, it takes less than two seconds to influence or impact another by simply *being* who you are.

In my quest to find out what exactly a person needs to bring to the table to be influential, the "power" comes from seven traits: confidence, commitment, courage, passion, empowering, trustworthiness, and likeability. I call them the Seven Influence Traits® and you've seen them referenced plenty in earlier chapters. These seven traits are identified as the qualities, characteristics, and assets that influential people possess. The exciting news? We all possess them.

The role these seven traits play in how influential you are is paramount to achieving success in all venues of the organization. It doesn't matter if you are the person on the line or sitting in the C-Suite. Everyone in an organization can be influential, in fact, they should be influential.

Several years ago, a large financial institution hired me to coach one of their executives, Victor, a knowledgeable, intelligent man who had great aspirations. The problem was he experienced a great deal of stress which began to interfere in his work. Victor was distracted, missing deadlines, and overall unhappy at work. After a few coaching sessions, we discovered he was doubting himself and losing confidence in his abilities at work, but it went deeper than that. Victor was losing confidence, period. He had just been promoted to a new position that demanded more from him. He couldn't understand why he was responding this way because this promotion was something he had been working toward for many years.

Victor described himself as hard-working, determined, having a purpose, and being a risk-taker. He couldn't understand what was wrong. When I pointed out that hard-working and determination come from commitment, having a purpose is about passion, and being a risk-taker centers around courage, he began to put the puzzle together. Victor had these traits in great supply but he wasn't maximizing them in his new position. Once he saw the bigger picture of his potential to impact or influence himself by leveraging these traits of commitment, passion, and courage, he took charge. Victor began to truly see himself fully being himself in his new position. He was able to show up as his influential self, not the doubting self. Victor's confidence grew and he was back on track even better than before.

In taking a look at the Seven Influence Traits® (confidence, commitment, courage, passion, empowering, trustworthiness, and likeability), you may feel you already understand what each trait represents, and of course you do to some degree, but you also need to see what it looks like when a person is deficient in these traits AND the effect it has on others around them. You will see that not developing your Seven Influence Traits® has direct consequences for you and an indirect impact on others around you, including (and especially) the organization.

Confidence in Motion

> *Do your very best, then let go of the outcome.*
>
> - DR. KAREN KELLER

Your mental attitude of believing in, trusting in and relying on yourself and your abilities is the greatest measure of your self-confidence. Self-assuredness in your own power and personal judgment is a strong indicator of self-confidence. Real self-confidence is present when you feel comfortable especially in situations with unknown outcome and uncertainty in general.

Confidence is a measure of the trust or faith you have in yourself and your abilities. It is the knowledge that you can succeed in a situation if you apply your skills to the important aspects of the task at hand.

True or ultimate self-confidence is accompanied by a "whatever it takes" attitude, where you promise yourself to try as hard as you can to reach your aspirations and goals, no matter how difficult it will be.

Impact of Low Confidence

Confidence is something most every person struggles with. When a person is deficient in confidence they appear self-centered, negative or insecure. They tend to rationalize their actions and shirk responsibility. Negativity overshadows their thinking which stands in the way of them giving their best. They begin to underestimate themselves on a regular basis.

The effect this has on others around them is that co-workers or team members start to feel discouraged, which breaks their spirit and affects the quality of their performance or work relationships. They avoid the low confidence person because they get tired of always needing to build him or her up. They feel exhausted and drained, which reduces the energy they have to give to their work.

One sign of a person with low confidence is they usually compare themselves to others. Richard was obsessed with what his co-workers were doing. What were they saying to the boss? Who was in their network? Why did they get the best projects? Richard was so focused on how he measured up to his "competition" that he neglected how he was doing. His confidence in who he was, what he was capable of, was overshadowed by always looking over the fence.

Power of Commitment

Making a worthwhile commitment requires it to be more than desirable. It has to be necessary.

- DR. KAREN KELLER

Commitment is the underlying force behind achievement. It is the single most determining factor as to whether you will receive all that is out there for you. Commitment is recognized by action. It is achieved without excuses, debate, or lengthy analysis.

Commitment represents a defined sense of purpose. Once that purpose is identified you are dedicated to it through your intention and action of furthering growth, learning and promise. You can only make a commitment to others when you have made a commitment to yourself first.

Impact of Low Commitment

Being deficient in the ability to make a commitment, either to yourself, to people in the organization, or to a new idea can show up as indifference. The person is seen as being distracted. He or she needs constant positive feedback. They tend to interpret failure as a reason to give up.

The effect this has on others is that they feel unworthy of the person's time and attention. They don't feel valued and it begins to affect their self-worth. There may be times when people around this person become frustrated or angry that due to the person's inability to make a commitment, they end up carrying the majority of the work load which leads to resentment.

Grant never gave much thought to how capable he was in making a commitment. But when it came down do it, Grant really wasn't that ambitious or motivated. He was basically a fence sitter. Grant was easily distracted by the shiny object in the room, and if it didn't exist, Grant would go looking for it. People in the company avoided Grant. Nobody would be on a team with him. They resented how Grant could just float along and nobody expected more of him.

Insights into Courage

Do it now or forever wish you had.

- DR. KAREN KELLER

Courage is your strength, power or determination to meet daunting circumstances head on. It is called upon whenever you meet a difficult, fear-provoking, painful or disturbing situation. You need courage when your resources are limited or pushed to the absolute edge or when you feel threatened, weak, vulnerable, intimidated or terrified.

Courage is doing the right thing in spite of fear. It is the foundation on which all other virtues and values rest. Courage is what helps you reach your deepest truth. It is from this truth that you make courageous choices. You need courage to act with confidence on your commitments to yourself and others.

Impact of Low Courage

When you lack courage, it results in stalled action or no action at all. You will go to great lengths to not take a risk. In fact, you usually say yes to everyone and everything because you do not have the courage to say no. The person who has low courage tends to give up easily.

The effect this has on people around them is that people don't feel heard. They continue asking for and expecting action to take place and when nothing happens, they believe you are ignoring them, or worse, that you don't care about their needs. They begin to view you as a person who is dismissing them and no longer sees them as bringing value to the company.

Emma couldn't make a decision if her life depended on it. She believed only in what she could see, in other words she believed she could only achieve the achievable. There was no room for risk, or pushing the limits. One day, Emma was faced with an opportunity to challenge a long held company view on a certain strategy. Personally, she thought it was time for a change, but she couldn't bring herself to disagree. She missed the chance to effect real change, to set a new direction.

Living with Passion

> *Work without passion is just work. Work with passion is food for the soul.*
>
> - DR. KAREN KELLER

Passion is a gift of your spirit united with the sum of all your life experiences. It affords you the power to live and communicate with unrestrained enthusiasm and eagerness. It is most apparent when your mind, body and spirit work together to create, develop and express your feelings, ideas and most sacred values. Passion creates energy -- an energy that's noticeable and transferable.

Passion enables you to overcome internal and external obstacles allowing you to see the world as a place of endless potential. Your passionate force looks at every event and discovers what can be, what should be and what will be.

Passion is a compelling emotion; intense emotional drive or excitement; and a strong liking, desire or devotion to an activity, object, or concept. So passion builds a state of strong desire.

Impact of Low Passion

Not having or communicating passion results in losing your sense of purpose. When you lose your sense of purpose your ability to focus suffers. You tend to move from project to project, not really accomplishing or bringing one thing to a conclusion. Having low passion also leads to little curiosity about things. You begin to only see things from one perspective.

The impact this has on others around you is they begin to sense that you've lost sight of *their* purpose. They start to think that you no longer see the big picture. That makes them believe you're not a partner in their journey to contribute to the big picture. When you show little interest in things (sans passion), they interpret that as you showing little interest in them.

Grace was so focused on "coloring inside the lines" that she showed little curiosity in anything else. Maintaining the status quo became her mission, possibly because routine became very comfortable. This affected Grace to the point where she wasn't much engaged in learning. She stopped asking why or why not. People were negatively affected by her loss of energy. Because of Grace's lack of passion for her job, for discovering new things, for challenging the status quo, she lost connection to other people.

Empowering with Purpose

Expecting the best from others raises the bar immensely.

- DR. KAREN KELLER

Empowering others is a practice of sharing information, rewards, and power with others so they can take initiative and make decisions to solve problems and improve their lives. It is based on the idea that when you give people the resources, authority, opportunity, and the chance to contribute, they will increase their competency and fulfillment.

Empowering others is a process that encourages people to gain control over their lives. It fosters power that they can use in all aspects of their lives. When you empower people you are helping them succeed and achieve on multiple levels. In short, empowering helps increase another person's spiritual, social, mental, and emotional strengths.

Impact of Low Empowering

When a person is deficient in empowering others, they appear as someone who is more interested in controlling the situation rather than exploring could be. It shows up as having little trust in others, doubting their competencies, and being somewhat oblivious to others' needs. The person who doesn't empower others tends to struggle with giving and receiving feedback.

The effect on others of a person who does not empower people is they begin to believe their vision is diminished. They start seeing themselves as only a cog in the great wheel that the low empowering person is controlling. Their creativity gets stymied. They begin to lose their passion for what they are doing. In essence, they feel as if they've been put in a box. And we all know that when we're in a box, not much innovation occurs.

Tom, Bob, Sharon, and Eli were on a team with Cheryl. To their dismay, Cheryl was the leader of the team. She provided direction, strategy, objectives, and the process to attain the goal. In other words, Cheryl did it all. Why? Because Cheryl was a control freak and perfectionist. Even though she could give great lip service to the other people on the team, her behavior was contrary. She really didn't believe they were as competent as she was. Cheryl rationalized it by saying she didn't want to be in a position where she had to clean up the team's messes or mistakes. She didn't see mistakes as a path to learning. As a result, the rest of the team didn't like Cheryl, and didn't respond to her. In fact, they disengaged, sat back, and watched her do all the work. She knew very little about empowering anyone.

Trustworthiness by Design

To be worthy of trust is one of the
highest achievements of a good life.

- DR. KAREN KELLER

Trustworthiness is a moral value considered to be a virtue. Being trustworthy means another person can place their trust in you and feel secure that their trust will not be betrayed. As a trustworthy person, you are honest, you keep your promises, and you value loyalty to others.

You prove your trustworthiness by accepting responsibility and meeting expectations. Your responsibility can be material, as in keeping a promise to pick up the dry cleaning, or non-material as in keeping an important secret. People find you trustworthy when you demonstrate your integrity over time.

Impact of Low Trustworthiness

If you are not trustworthy, you will show up as arrogant and vague because you aren't transparent. You don't subscribe to compromising or being consistent. You tend to hedge your bets, always looking out for where you can get the "best deal." Therefore people find you manipulative or intimidating. They will be cautious or hesitant to get to know you or share anything of importance.

The impact the untrustworthy person has on others is that people begin to withdraw first from the person, then from the organization. Lacking trust in your co-workers is something that easily and quite often transitions to not trusting the organization. People then shut down. They become guarded and skeptical. Eventually they separate from the organization.

Emma, who was responsible for human resource activities in the company, didn't trust easily. She tended to play her cards close to the chest, i.e., people thought she held back, was judgmental, and fairly superficial. They didn't experience Emma as being very flexible and not showing much compassion for their situations. Imagine the impact this had on people needing support from HR. People started going around Emma. They didn't trust that she could handle their concerns. Because this set up a distrusting environment, people's morale plummeted. They subscribed more to gossip about Emma over believing they had a supporter in HR.

Likeability in Action

> *Unexpected kindness is the most powerful, least costly, and most underrated agent of human change.*

> \- DR. KAREN KELLER

Likeability is a measure of how positively you are viewed by another person. It is also one of the most ignored factors of being successful and happy. Likeability is evidence by *how a person feels about him or herself when they are with you.* Your likeability depends on your ability to create positive attitudes in other people through the delivery of emotional and physical benefits. If you are highly likeable, it is predicted that you will bring people joy, put them at ease and reap the benefits of a loyal friendship.

Impact of Low Likeability

This trait is the "gateway" trait because if you aren't approachable, people will never see what you have to offer them. If you are not likeable you can appear to be superficial or aloof. People see you as not being a good listener, being judgmental, or perhaps being sarcastic, which you see as having a sense of humor.

The impact this has on others is they end up feeling disrespected. They don't feel good about themselves when they are around you. If they leave after a conversation with you feeling down, negative, or hopeless, then their brain attributes those feelings to you, where they interpret that to mean you aren't the most likeable person, so they tend to avoid and ignore you. If they leave their conversation with you feeling excited, energized, and positive about themselves, they attribute all those great feelings to you. Therefore they see you as being likeable.

Ken took himself seriously, too seriously. There wasn't any room for error or laughing at his own shortcomings. He invested a lot of time in protecting himself, but his co-workers were never certain from what. Ken didn't particularly find people interesting. Actually he became quite bored when listening to people talk about their lives. Now, the sad part was Ken thought nobody noticed how he truly felt. It was blatantly apparent to everyone but Ken. People went out of their way to avoid him. They didn't include him in after-hour activities. As a result Ken became lonely and isolated at work.

The Seven Influence Traits®

The importance of these traits run deep throughout the organization from the individual person, to the impact they have in the team environment, to the very heart of the organizational culture. It's like a small trickle that turns into a stream, emerging into a raging river, and emptying into the vast ocean.

Building successful companies, business, and organizational communities all starts with each individual person's ability to maximize these Seven Influence Traits® for the good of the organization. You can see how detrimental it is to lack these traits.

Developing your influence potential is the first step in creating shifts that are necessary in an organization to not only sustain long term performance and growth, but to establish a strong culture that is based on how each person impacts another person, i.e., their internal customer.

What difference will it make to invest in an employee to develop their confidence or likeability or any of these traits? It makes all the difference. Consider what your organization would look like and how your customers would be affected if all confidence and likeability were removed from every person in your company. What impact would that have? How long would it take to be noticed? A nano-second.

How would your company look or how would people show up if each person had one hundred percent confidence or trustworthiness? How would that impact the company? Beyond words.

Looking at influence through this lens helps people understand the importance of building their Seven Influence Traits®. This is seeing a new dimension of ourselves. Being influential is the foundation of everything. It's the difference between success and failure. It's the source of prosperous change. It's the initial stage of connection. And it's the pathway to having the ultimate impact on others.

As Tom Peters, author of *In Search of Excellence,* said,

"Never underestimate the importance of the basics." He was right. The basics for being an influential person, who doesn't rely on tips and tricks, is the person who grows, embraces, and masters their confidence, commitment, courage, passion, empowering, trustworthiness, and likeability. This is what people respond to. This is what opens doors. And this is what creates great influential leaders.

Influence Lives Everywhere Including Finding Solutions

Carl Fisher was a problem solver his entire life. Most people solve problems to gain riches and fame. That wasn't Carl's motivation. Carl solved problems because that was in his nature. Opening a car dealership during the boom of the auto industry, Carl realized that people would want to drive at night, so he invented headlights. Next, Carl thought that people would want to race their cars. So, Carl built a race track. The racetrack is now known as the Indy 500. Carl saw a bridge being built in Florida from a resort area to some swamp land. He made a deal with the bridge builder that he would help build a better bridge if he could have the swamp land on the other side. Carl turned this swamp land into Miami Beach. Carl invented and built things because he had to solve a problem and improve the world, not because he wanted to become rich and famous, (although he did make millions) but because he wanted to make a difference.

This is what you want to have in common with Carl. You want to make a difference. In your life, in the lives of others, and in your organization.

When it comes to problems, the first step to solving them is to change them. Change your perspective, change the meaning, and change how you usually approach a problem. Change your level of influence. Use your Seven Influence Traits® to your advantage.

Finding solutions, the best solutions, relies heavily on your confidence to believe in your ability to solve the problem, your commitment to not be deterred, and your courage to ask tough questions. It depends on your passion to inspire those around you, your ability to empower diverse ideas and possibilities, your trustworthiness to be dependable, and your likeable nature. All these traits, the Seven Influence Traits®, are instrumental in attaining greater awareness and answers in a competitive environment.

Here's the BEST NEWS

My dad always told me, "You are the best asset you will ever have." He was right.

You are the first resource that needs to be uncovered. You are the best resource available. You are your best asset, so start with you. You own each of the Seven Influence Traits®. You need to identify where they are strong, which traits need work, and how you will maximize and leverage them in becoming an influential person.

Every problem can be solved or changed by using a combination of your influence traits – ideally all of them. The combination and strength of your Seven Influence Traits® are instrumental in gauging how well you will meet any obstacle in your way.

For example, when you meet with your boss and you

feel the lump in your throat, the perspiration under your shirt, and the fogginess in your head, it's your confidence that says, "Hey wait a minute, I have something to offer – and it is good!" It's your courage that proclaims, "Move over, here I come!" It's your likeability and trustworthiness that says, "Yes, let's hear what he has to say."

As you look at being influential and how to grow these traits, know that there are multiple opportunities that exist every minute of every day, whether you're influencing yourself or someone else or your environment or a decision. It's always there. Once you see your life through this new lens, it will change your perspective and your results tremendously.

This is what makes this new perspective on influence so powerful. It comes with a guarantee. When you identify a problem, issue, concern, worry, or a success, a win, or something that is going right, I guarantee all of this can be traced back to one or more of these seven traits. That's how powerful and effective they are. Every person on this planet has each of these Seven Influence Traits®. The only difference between a middle of the road influencer and a great influencer is how each nurture and capitalize on their traits.

From today on you have the opportunity to actually use your Seven Influence Traits® regardless of your circumstances because these traits all exist within you.

Influence belongs to some; being influential belongs to everyone. Not everyone has money, title, position, or authority, but everyone has the traits of confidence, commitment, courage, passion, empowering, trustworthiness, and likeability. The thing that makes some people more influential than others is simply the strongest degree of and the way they use or maximize each of these traits. Before you can maximize an influence trait you need to know how much of it you actually have. (We're getting to that.)

It is that simple. However, it is not easy. We've grown up knowing these seven words, but it can be scary to talk about your confidence, or to find out you aren't as likeable as you thought you were. It's tough to learn how to express your passion, or make a commitment with depth and strength. But people are doing it. And so can you.

Once you grow your seven traits, others will notice you and they will appreciate the value you bring to the table. And the benefit of that? Less stress. Healthy bottom lines. Better relationships. More satisfaction. Greater identity. And . . . more influence.

What happens when your Seven Influence Traits® are not functioning on all cylinders? People

- Walk all over you
- Dismiss your ideas
- Ignore you
- Don't notice you
- Won't follow you
- Offer you no help
- Won't endorse or refer to you

Failing to grow your influence – not capitalizing on your Seven Influence Traits® – leads to a life of disappointment where you end up asking over and over again, "Why not me? What are they doing that I'm not? What am I missing?"

In the organization, the questions become: "What are

we missing?" "Why is engagement low in our organization?" "What happened to morale and trust?" "How are others doing it?" "Why are we not leading in our market?" How often are these little scenarios repeated in your life?

- Your ideas spark a niche in the market, but someone else gets the credit.
- You know there is an opportunity around the corner, but you keep on walking.
- The vast knowledge you have on XYZ goes unnoticed because everyone else is drowning you out.
- You witness the great lunches your co-workers are going to... but you have a cold sandwich at your desk day after day.

Your life can be better than this. Once you take full advantage of every influence trait you have, identifying where they are, discovering how to make them work for you, and getting rid of what is holding you back, you will experience attention, respect, and response from everyone in your life.

And that's the power of self-influence. When you influence yourself first, build your confidence, expand your passion, empower others, or become more likeable, the world sees you as a different person. In fact, they more than see you, they want to hear, follow and experience you, too.

Now that's real influence! Getting people to want to listen to you, to want to encourage you and to want to help you... it doesn't get much better than that.

Confidence Checklist

- ☐ I do what I love.
- ☐ I am optimistic about my life.
- ☐ I live my core values.
- ☐ I say aloud my personal positive affirmation.
- ☐ I take action in spite of my fear.
- ☐ I surround myself with confident people.
- ☐ I listen to positive self-talk.
- ☐ I act according to my guiding principles.
- ☐ I appreciate my talents and skills.
- ☐ I laugh often.
- ☐ I create extraordinary differences.

Commitment Checklist

- ☐ I explore things I don't know.
- ☐ I listen to other viewpoints.
- ☐ I am decisive.
- ☐ I see the big picture.
- ☐ I ask questions.
- ☐ I learn about my competition.
- ☐ I measure pain against pleasure.
- ☐ I entertain my objections.
- ☐ I refrain from making assumptions.
- ☐ I engage in a creative process.
- ☐ I will teach someone something new each day.

Courage Checklist

☐ I do not retreat.

☐ I trust myself.

☐ I engage with character.

☐ I practice humility.

☐ I initiate action.

☐ I help others.

☐ I assess my faults.

☐ I stand up for myself.

☐ I believe in solving problems.

☐ I find new perspectives.

☐ I manage through courage roadblocks.

Passion Checklist

- ☐ I live my best possible life.
- ☐ I have a try-again attitude.
- ☐ I am driven by results.
- ☐ I work on things close to my heart.
- ☐ I give 100%.
- ☐ I use my inner creativity
- ☐ I am motivated to succeed.
- ☐ I motivate other people.
- ☐ I always take the next step.
- ☐ I bring energy to what I do.
- ☐ I love to have fun.

Empowering Checklist

- ☐ I create alignment among people.
- ☐ I build support for the vision.
- ☐ I comfortably share power.
- ☐ I encourage other people to make decisions.
- ☐ I nurture talent in others.
- ☐ I provide opportunities.
- ☐ I know there is more I can learn.
- ☐ I can let go.
- ☐ I share my knowledge and resources.
- ☐ I focus on strengths.
- ☐ I expect the best from people.

Trustworthiness Checklist

☐ I follow through with my promises.

☐ I tell the truth.

☐ I can take emotional risks.

☐ I am authentic.

☐ I act with integrity.

☐ I am compassionate.

☐ I like to build connection.

☐ My actions match my words.

☐ My ethics are consistent.

☐ I accept differences between others

 and myself.

☐ I believe in fairness.

Likeability Checklist

☐ I am interested in other people.

☐ I am a secure person.

☐ I don't judge people.

☐ I provide value.

☐ I am happy for other people's success.

☐ I am sincere.

☐ I give second chances.

☐ I learn from my mistakes.

☐ I am approachable.

☐ I acknowledge other people.

☐ I love to laugh and laugh often.

Transitioning from Influence to Influential

A burning desire is the starting point of all triumph. Just like a small fire cannot give much heat, a weak desire cannot produce great results.

- ANONYMOUS

To accept a truth that challenges or changes your perspective requires a certain humility. Getting a new insight is not just adding something to a list. It affects the other truths you hold, just as the birth of a new child affects *everything* the whole family does. That is why oftentimes people or organizations close their minds. They fear the chain reaction a new insight might have on everything else. But a closed mind is a prison. The truth will set you free.

A young man asked Socrates the secret to success. Socrates asked the young man to walk with him into the river. When the water got up to their necks, Socrates took the young man by surprise and dunked him into the water. The young man struggled to get out but Socrates was strong and kept him there until he started turning blue.

When Socrates pulled him up, the first thing the young man did was gasp and take a deep breath of air. Socrates asked: "What did you want the most when you were there?"

The young man replied: "Air."

Socrates said: "That is the secret to success. When you want success as badly as you wanted the air, then you will get it. There is no other secret."

It is only when you are truly thirsty for knowledge, wisdom, or opportunity that you are willing to really put yourself out there to gain all that is waiting for you. You come to a point in life where you realize there is more you want, but what are you willing to do to get it? To bring it into your life? To bring it into your organization?

Napoleon Hill wrote: "Whenever the mind of man can conceive and believe, the mind can achieve." The motivation to succeed comes from the burning desire to achieve a purpose.

What can organizations do to move from a "having influence" mindset to a "being influential" mindset?

Listen.

We need to listen to each other, to get to the meaning behind the words. There are three ways we listen. First, we listen with our ears. We hear the words and filter them through our own experience. We tend to stop hearing midway through and start planning or preparing how we are going to respond. Second, we listen with our eyes. Listening with our eyes is when we take in the facial expressions, the body language and gesture. We get closer to understanding what is important to the person talking. We need to refrain from judging what we see. And lastly, the third way of listening is with our hearts. That is when we listen to what isn't being said. We strive to "hear" the emotions that give birth to the words, to the body's expressions. We make a concerted effort to make an emotional connection to the other person without dismissing or judging them.

Listening is the only way we can find answers to our questions. An influential organization (and individual) has to be willing to truly listen. The organization's true potential is found in the collection of the most creative insights from the people that make up the organization. Every organization can seek and find talent. New sources of information and knowledge come from the people in the organization. The problem many organizations run into is how they access that information and knowledge. The only requirement for listening to what people can tell them is the organization's willingness to do so.

Finding My Own Influential Power

In the spring of 1997, while I was away completing a clinical residency at a psychiatric hospital, my life took an unexpected detour. The Red River in my hometown in Northern Minnesota became a true force of nature. Because of the eighteen feet of winter snow, a three-day ice storm, and a two-day white out blizzard followed by a few days of warm weather, the river banks could not contain the enormous rapid thaw. Man-made dikes were destroyed by the river's expansion which grew to be miles wide.

From 950 miles away, I watched the town I grew up in evacuated in 48 hours. My daughters, who were staying with my parents, were carried out by the National Guard in three feet of water. My father had a massive stroke. My mother, who also was hospitalized had her first, and last, helicopter ride when they evacuated the hospital. I felt helpless and scared. The river rose so high it covered the chimneys of many homes.

I watched this horrible disaster destroy everything including my home. It was a slow painful process to watch over a period of days. Nothing would be the same. Life as I knew it was gone. My plan to return to open a clinical practice was gone. The direction of my entire life changed – forever.

However, if it weren't for the natural disaster that crossed my path, I wouldn't have gone on to save lives, I wouldn't be a thought leader in my industry, and I wouldn't have discovered my own influential force. And I probably wouldn't have written this book telling you that you have the personal potential and power to influence the direction of your own life.

That flood was responsible for placing me where I am today. I was left without a home, no job, and two young children to take care of. Even though this river changed the course of my life – it empowered me to influence my future.

This experience forced me to acknowledge my passion for what I did – help people who suffered from severe mental illness. I wanted to make a difference and was willing to do whatever it took to succeed. I was, and still am, passionate.

Acknowledging this passion gave rise to my courage. I had to muster all my courage to start completely over in a new place. No family, not many belongings, but I had me and my girls. Courage is my favorite trait because as Maya Angelou said, *"Women must first develop courage. Courage is the most important of all virtues because without courage, they cannot practice any other virtue consistently. A woman can be kind, fair, strong, generous, courteous and even loving, erratically. But to be that continuously, you have to have courage."* It was my courage that forced me to not only accept my fate but forge ahead to create my destiny.

The next trait that emerged was my confidence. I knew I'd make mistakes but I believed in myself. It's interesting how the things you hear as a child really do stick with you. As I mentioned earlier, my dad always told me, "Karen, you are the best asset you have. Never forget that." More than ever before, his words were front and center in my mind. It was a strong sense of confidence that pushed me to take on my new challenge and persist through setbacks. My confidence was my greatest support when I felt uncertain and when I was told no.

Next, I realized that to continue on my path, I had to commit to the outcome no matter where it led me. This is where confidence and courage partnered in knowing that I had to push through my situation and that I could get through it. I was committed. It was similar to Scarlett O'Hara's famous words in *Gone With The Wind*, "As God is my witness, I'll never be hungry again." Did I go hungry? No. But there were lots of mac and cheese nights! My point is that I was so determined to provide a secure life for my children that I was completely committed and focused to do whatever it took to meet their needs and build a happy life for my family. I integrate and maximize all seven traits now in my work - in working with individuals, teams, organizations, and in training coaches to use the Keller

Influence Indicator® (KII®) Program I developed.

The Life Impact of the Seven Influence Traits®

Consider for a second the traits that inspired some of the greatest figures in history. For example, confidence is what kept Beethoven composing even though his teacher said he had no musical talent. Courage is what made Colonel Sanders continue pitching his chicken recipe after 1002 rejections. Passion for a crazy idea is what kept Walt Disney going after he was turned down by one hundred banks for his "mouse" idea.

Commitment is what allowed Thomas Edison to invent even after he was told he was '"too stupid to learn." Empowering himself to succeed is what pushed Fred Astaire to continue dancing after a director said "he can't act and he can only dance a little." These traits are part of every influential leader today. Confidence is what drove Ursula Burns to rise from a poor, black, single-parent family to become the CEO of XEROX.

Nurturing the Seven Influence Traits® was the difference between success and failure for all of these people. It was their passion, or their ability to empower themselves, that led them to achieve more than anyone would have thought possible. These traits influenced their attitude, their willingness to continue, and their ability to focus on what they wanted. What they learned was that when people respond to who you are, ninety-nine percent of the time people respond to what you do.

My Personal Transition

Several years ago, I had the opportunity to hear Zig Ziglar speak at a conference. It was toward the end of his career, but he still had the magic of his early years. His message was inspirational. But there was something more I heard in his voice. He relayed a message of be who you are. Don't try to be anyone else or who others think you should be. If you do, you'll miss the boat every time. This was important to me because I was in major career transition once again. I had to make the decision to leave the solid clinical practice I had built or pursue a career in executive coaching. I was torn and spent many sleepless nights pondering this decision. During Zig's speech, I believed he was talking directly to me. (But then again, I also thought Paul McCartney blew me a kiss during his concert, so I digress).

I heard what I needed to hear. It was time to move forward with a bigger desire. It would be hard, risky, and could potentially fail, but I needed to try. The week following the conference I made the decision to close my practice and strike out in the world of executive coaching.

What did it take for me to make this transformation?

The new path I was taking was more than another chapter in my life. It was a major transition to something greater that would force me to stretch, question, and reach. It would make me conquer whatever fears would hold me back. I had to resist the temptation to be distracted by all the other thoughts and opportunities. I had to follow my passion. It also required that I expand my Seven Influence Traits®.

J.K. Rowling describes her life as a "mess" before Harry Potter. She was a single parent on welfare, depressed, just lost her mother, totally down and out. BUT she was committed to one thing – writing her children's stories. After hitting rock bottom and twelve publishers who turned down her manuscript, things changed. Because of a little girl named Alice Newton. Alice was the daughter of the Chairman of the Board for a small publishing house named Bloomsbury. Because of Alice Newton's excitement over JK Rowling's stories, we now have Harry Potter. Because of JK Rowling's passion and commitment, we have a whole new world of wizardry and magic. You may not ever meet Ms. Rowling, but she has influenced fans across the globe.

Putting yourself out there, being a beacon of light for others, impacting or influencing people in your daily life and perhaps some you will never meet is one of the greatest achievements you will have when you become influential. Reading this book thus far has already got you on the right track. Now let's go further.

Chapter Eight Checklist

- ☐ You are the best asset you will ever have.

- ☐ A burning desire is the secret to all success.

- ☐ Strive to hear the emotions.

- ☐ You are the first resource that needs to be uncovered.

- ☐ Nurture your Seven Influence Traits® every day.

- ☐ Force yourself to stretch, question, and reach.

- ☐ Put yourself out there. Be a beacon of light.

- ☐ Being influential means you are able to connect as a human being.

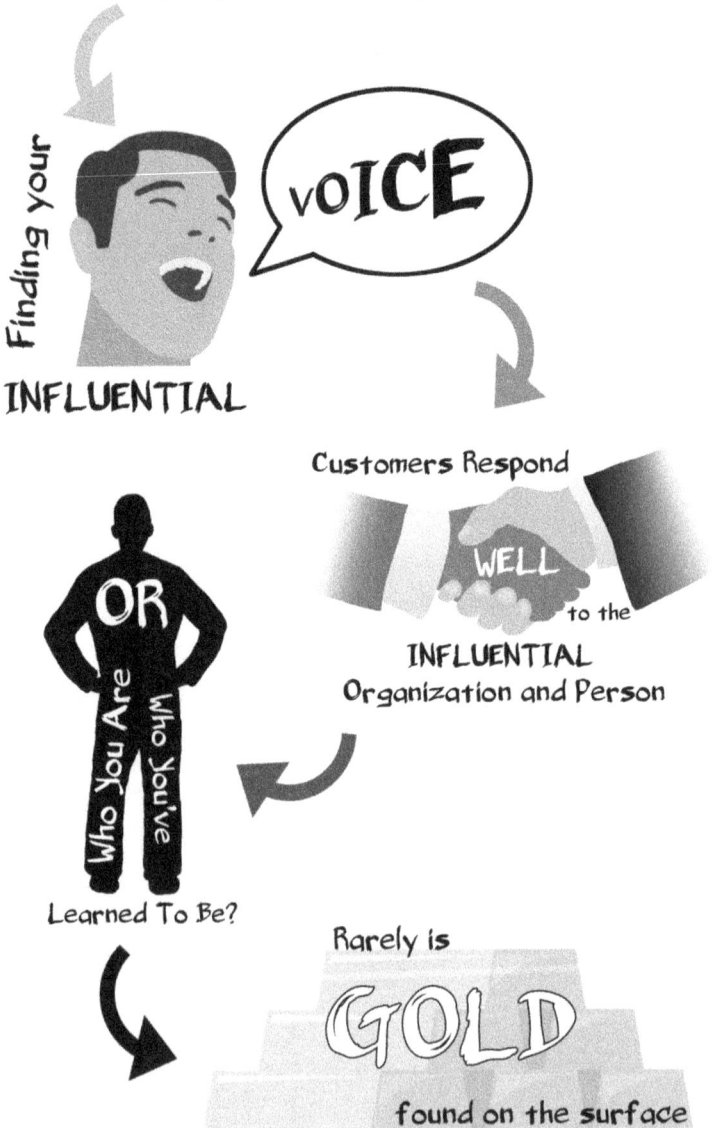

CHAPTER NINE

What Are You Waiting For?

Whatever must happen ultimately should happen immediately.

- HENRY KISSINGER

A great example of courage is Asma Jahangir, the founder of Pakistan's first all-female law firm and President of the Supreme Court Bar Association of Pakistan. Because she fearlessly challenges human rights abuses, her home has been broken into, she and her family have been attacked, taken hostage, and received death threats daily. Jahangir was imprisoned for standing up for human rights, but that didn't deter her from doing what needed to be done. She continues to be a voice for men, women and children who are not allowed to speak. Asma Jahangir is a great example of courage on a grand scale.

We also have what I call everyday courage which is equally important. Everyday courage is the constant presence of resolution when we decide to learn something new, speak out, defend right, or share our vulnerabilities.

Everyday courage has no witnesses. It doesn't get awards or standing ovations or headlines. It takes courage to act with confidence on your commitments. And these are acts we perform every day. From questioning an overcharge on a bill or an undeserved grade on a project to delivering an unpopular but necessary report to the board of directors or making a critical decision in the operating room, it all takes courage.

Once you begin growing, understanding, and using your Seven Influence Traits®, you will experience a new view of yourself. You will begin to see the role these traits play in your ability to learn, to feel, *and to take action.*

Scott, a marketing coordinator for an international brewery franchise, was recently promoted and assigned to develop a new multi-level social media strategy for the company's customer outreach. Scott came to this position having specific experience in design, branding strategies, relationship building, writing, image, analytics, and public relations. He believed this would be his breakout moment, a time when he could really make a difference, build positive networks, and be recognized for his talent and skills.

Scott had been working in his new position for just over seven weeks, and soon became overwhelmed and stressed out¬¬¬¬¬¬¬—not because of his promotion or the switch in work-related tasks, but because of his new boss, Rick. Rick, Director of Marketing, delineated responsibilities and tasks for Scott to complete, however, he consistently "flip-flopped" about the required tasks, micromanaged Scott's work, and never gave him necessary feedback.

Rick had the habit of belittling Scott's emails during the early morning rap sessions with other team members, making decisions on Scott's work without reviewing anything with him, and pointing the finger at Scott when the results weren't what he wanted. Scott was uncertain about how to deal with the situation. He loved his job. He felt he could move the company's online presence and profile to a new level, but the stress of his boss was making it extremely difficult. Scott constantly worried about his job performance (these thoughts kept him up at night), and he found himself working overtime and at the expense of his other responsibilities, both work related and personal. Scott knew that in order to succeed in his new position, something needed to change, and fast. But he felt like he had cement in his shoes keeping him downright stuck.

The company was my client. They retained me to see what was "going on" with Scott. Scott felt he had no way out and had begun looking for another position with the competition. Scott felt he couldn't trust Rick. I immediately worked with Scott on a plan to change his circumstances. He identified what needed to be done, what he wasn't doing, and what barriers he would need to address to make progress.

The first thing Scott noted was his inability to have a conversation with Rick due to Rick's manipulative and somewhat intimidating nature. Scott realized he lacked the courage to confront Rick's behavior. He also admitted that he was losing his commitment to the job. What Scott didn't grasp until now was how these circumstances were removing his passion and influencing how he came across to others. Scott realized he was mostly in a bad mood, developing a bad attitude, not paying attention to other people's needs, wanting to leave work early; basically, Scott didn't care anymore.

It's important to see how Rick's lack of these traits impacted Scott's behavior. Another thing to notice is since

Scott's Seven Influence Traits® were not well developed, he was left vulnerable to Ricks' behavior. One step further, Scott then behaved poorly toward others. So do you now see how not developing employee's ability to be influential (their Seven Influence Traits®) has a serious trickle down impact within an organization?

With the appropriate influence coaching sessions, Scott decided to become stronger in his Seven Influence Traits® and increase his awareness of when and how to use them. He developed the confidence and courage to address the entire situation with Rick. The outcome was Scott was given responsibilities independent of Rick's influence and the company realized they had a new problem to deal with - Rick.

What we can learn from Scott's (and Rick's) situation is that the power of being influential is the cornerstone for every dynamic, circumstance, decision, action, response, and idea at an organization. The source of being a great influencer is more than just doing, or persuading – it's being influential. Being influential knows no boundaries. It is the single most important asset an employee and an organization can possess.

Finding Your Influential Voice

Only those who will risk going too far can possibly find out how far one can go.

- T.S. ELIOT

Each of us has a voice. What we need to learn is to listen to our influential voice.

The ACME Company sells widgets, all sizes, shapes, and colors to many different customers. Team XYZ is in charge of inventory and has been "functioning" for more than a year. Max is always in charge (no shared leadership exists here), and Amy and Perry usually find a way to manipulate Max to get what they want. The other team members just go along to avoid any confrontation or conflict. One day, a new person joined the team, Evan.

Evan came from an organization that practiced shared leadership, truth-telling, and acting according to the core values of both himself and the company. During Evan's first team meeting, Amy and Perry were "convincing" Max that ordering more than the usual amount of material for widget ABC was the best thing to do. They told Max that this would make less work down the road, less record keeping. Of course Max was eager to do anything that would make his job easier. And the rest of the team didn't say a word. In fact, they praised Max's decision. However, Evan spoke up and said, "This isn't a good idea. Ordering more than this project needs has a high possibility of ending up as scrap, costing the ACME Company millions of dollars and wasted coveted storage space." The team gasped, looking at him as if he had horns. Max was embarrassed. Amy and Perry were angry.

Evan was being influential. He demonstrated confidence, courage, and commitment to what was in the best interests of the company. While Amy and Perry were "influencing," the rest of the team ignored the influence or impact they might have had on Max.

Evan found and used his influential voice. He had the courage to move in the opposite direction from the group. He listened to his gut. His influential voice was longing to create, to share, to explore, and connect.

Being influential is not about finding the right words, rather it centers on finding a wrong and making it right. It can mean creating something out of nothing. It can mean acting on the deep impulse to make the world a better place. When you find your influential voice, you find a little more freedom to speak, express, and to let yourself be heard. Your influential voice is supported by your confidence, your passion, and your capacity to empower.

This is what customers respond to over and over again.

Imagine how an organization would function if everyone found and used their influential voice. It will lead to a communication process where people are free to be genuine and authentic with each other. People will listen and be patient with each other. They will feel secure in disagreeing because they share the same purpose. They will develop trust in depending on each other, while still competing for the best ideas. Finding your influential voice means finding a way to express your ideas so that you connect with other people. When people develop their influential voice, and bring forth their different experiences and knowledge, the brand and reputation of the organization reveals a community that thrives on integrity and value.

Organizations who nurture a person's passion or courage pays huge dividends. Why? Because every single person the employee interacts with is touched by their passion or their courage. Passion ignites passion in other people. Courage ignites courage in other people. On the other hand, if the organization ignores the negative, perfectionistic, or lazy person, this, too, impacts other people. But more like a nasty infection. Which would you rather have? Where would you rather work?

Every person can transition from having influence to being influential. Moving from having influence to being influential is a transformation. It requires moving from having influence to being influential is a transformation. The big difference between highly influential people and those that want to be is the time they commit to getting prepared.

Who You Are or Who You've Learned to Be?

We all start out with what we've been given. Actually, I believe that anyone under six years old is blessed with the greatest confidence, courage, passion, commitment, and likeability. All you need to do is watch children play – nothing gets in the way of simply being who they are.

Then there is the other scenario – who we've learned to be. That's where our potential, in this case, our Seven Influence Traits® become affected by our environment, parents, teachers, and peers, or playmates. We acquiesce to expectations, react with disappointment to not being recognized, or shrivel under looming dominance. On the other hand, we may have the opportunity to blossom from praise, rebound when offered support, and dare to be more. There comes a point in everyone's life where we veer from being who we are to becoming someone we've learned to be.

Becoming who we are could be a reaction for survival, or it could be a response to acknowledgement. In either case, we take our cue from people around us. And hence, our Seven Influence Traits® will either flourish or deteriorate. We can become more authentic or be left to search for how to fit into a world that doesn't notice us.

Human Capital

Responsibility is a sign of trust.
Accountability is a sign of confidence.

- DR. KAREN KELLER

We hear so much about human capital. But what is human capital really? It sounds like something on the stock exchange that can be bought and sold. That was how traditional methods of influence have operated in the past. Human capital is more than the skills, knowledge or experience that employees offer to a company. Looking at it this way almost makes an excuse for organizations to treat humans as a commodity. There is usually an emphasis on getting people to "do" all the time. Of course, if action doesn't take place nothing gets done, but let's dig a little deeper. It's kind of like looking for gold. Rarely is gold found on the surface.

Although all skills, knowledge and experience are part of human capital, there is a more comprehensive look needed when it comes to evaluating what a person is really worth. We need to look at what they bring to the table. How they show up. What makes one employee more valuable than another, aside from the skills difference? It's how influential they are. It's how they treat another person on the job. It's how they respond or communicate truth. It's how they help others. And it's how they see themselves as being valuable contributors to the success of a company.

Organizations need to stop and actually look at their people. Who are they? How do we get to know them? How well do they know themselves? That is the place to start: How well do the people in an organization know themselves? Are they placing worth on who they are or do they find themselves in a never-ending cycle of jumping through hoops to do this or do that?

People in our organizations begin to feel like lab rats trying to find their way out of a maze, always striving for the carrot in front of them. What to do better, how to contribute more, where to get the best ideas, and the list marches on. Just imagine the pressure that builds even in the best at a company. What we are describing are human *doings*.

Organizations tend to forget about the *being* part, probably because that is somewhat intangible. It's hard to get our arms around a personality, or a particular way of seeing the world. Yes, companies are looking at personality, attitude, and style as it pertains to organizational behaviors, but where is it taking us? When we try to coach or instill a specific type of personality we are messing with the natural order of a person's makeup. It is akin to the Westminster Kennel Club dog shows. The contestants are well groomed, spectacular at worst, but the one thing that nobody would ever attempt to change is the personality of a pedigree. That's what makes them stand out. That's what wins the Best in Show.

So, what should we pay attention to in our organizations? Yes, the people, but what about the people? When was the last time you heard someone share with you about their courage? Do you remember a time when an executive mentioned how committed they were to the goals of the organization? Has anyone ever discussed their likeability or trustworthiness with you? Probably not lately. Of course, we know about courage and commitment, but most people generally don't see themselves as committed or courageous. They see themselves as a behavior, like "he follows instruction well" or "she embraces opportunities."

Johan Wolfgang von Goethe said, "Treat a man as he appears to be and you make him worse. But treat a man as if he already were what he potentially could be, and you make him what he should be."

People are more than their behaviors. Organizations need to find what is behind those behaviors. You want people to know their potential to be influential. Close your eyes and imagine what you could accomplish if you had all the confidence in the world, or were a person whom everyone liked, trusted and respected.

The Benefit of Having Abundance in the Seven Influence Traits®

A former client of mine, Connor, was a Senior VP of operations in his company. He told me how when it came to his work, he knows what he's doing. He feels secure that his education prepared him. Connor confidently relied on being able to apply his great wealth of experience to everything he did . . . at work. But when it came to raising his three teenage boys, he had the greatest doubts in the world. He expressed that he didn't feel prepared, had no experience, in other words, he said he didn't have any confidence in what he is doing as a parent. "It's like shooting in the dark!"

So I asked Connor, "What do you do as a parent of three teenage boys who has never done this before?" He told me he depends on his wife. He reads books and current articles on raising boys and teenagers by authors who have a solid track record. He talks to friends who have already raised teenagers – successfully. He keeps the conversation open. He builds the relationship by spending time with the boys together and individually. He said, "I trust my instincts. I have a high regard for common sense, but I also have a high regard for what's right and wrong as well as something outside the box. I want to instill solid values in them so when I'm not around they make good choices." All I had to say was, "Spoken like a confident person."

The point of this story is to show you that when your Seven Influence Traits® are high, they can be transitioned to any situation, especially the situations or circumstances where you feel uncomfortable and totally out of your element. In fact, these situations are *where you need these traits most.* Tough situations are where your confidence or courage, for example, show up to serve and support you. Everyone finds themselves in new surroundings, with new people, confronted with new ideas, and it's our Seven Influence Traits® that keeps us grounded and open to new ways or people, where we can enjoy the newness without feeling stressed or incompetent.

Your Seven Influence Traits® are the fuel that determines how you approach everything. It doesn't mean you have all the answers. It doesn't mean you have no naggings of doubt. It does mean you have the ability to use your resources. You ask those tough questions that get you over the fence of uncertainty. You put fear in the drawer because you know you need to go forward. This is why it is critical that you consistently nurture your Seven Influence Traits®. It's not, "Do I have all the answers?" It's about, "Am I willing to find those answers?" That's the difference between the influential person and the person who isn't.

When you find and embrace your Seven Influence

Traits®, you have the capacity to move forward, removing those self-limiting conversations that prevent you from experiencing fulfillment. The impact this has on others is they want to know what you know. They want to hear your message and learn about your ideas. They're going to follow you. They're going to trust you. You become the person who can walk into the room and say or do nothing and still be influential.

The Influential Mindset

In many ways, being influential is about your brand or reputation, it comes before you. If you give another person an experience of you as a confident, self-assured individual, they walk away having that memory, having an experience of you being a confident person. So when they see you next, guess what happens? When they hear you speaking out on an issue, when they hear you contributing a new ideas during a team meeting, what do they do? What do they believe? They see you has having influence, as being influential. Not because of anything you've DONE, but because you gave them an experience of WHO you are. This is when they listen to your ideas. They are willing to adopt a new way of thinking or action.

It is so important to be influential. Every individual has the opportunity to affect change in their world. You want to make a difference. You want to make your world better, whether it's the world inside the walls of your house or organization or the world inside your church or in your school or in your community or in your country. That's the power of being influential. It goes with you everywhere.

Chapter Nine Checklist

- ☐ Everyday courage is the constant presence of resolution. Everyone has it.

- ☐ It takes courage to act with confidence on your commitments.

- ☐ You need to listen to your influential voice.

- ☐ Organizations who nurture a person's passion or courage reap huge dividends.

- ☐ Two choices: who you are and who you've learned to be.

- ☐ Responsibility is a sign of trust. Accountability is a sign of confidence.

- ☐ Being influential is about your brand or reputation.

CHAPTER TEN

Righting the Wrong

When there's an elephant in the room, introduce him.

- RANDY PAUSCH
Former professor, Carnegie Mellon University

Our organizations and our people are breaking. They're crumbling under the pressure of always having to do more, faster, better, and deliver yesterday. Technology is setting the expectation that people need to be superhuman to get the job done. The frustration intensified a few years ago with the ideal of work/life balance being the hot button issue yet nobody knew what real work/life balance was. So we said it was time management. Time for work, time to play, time for family. The problem was while we were playing at home or elsewhere, we were still looking at our tablets and smart phones because we didn't want to be left behind at work. We worried that John or Joan would get the chance to present, or an opportunity to be heard, or the next promotion. Take a vacation to maintain that work/life balance? Sure, but vacations became working vacations. One eye on our kid in the pool and one eye scrolling the phone.

So then we developed the notion and slogan to "unplug." That was interesting. We pretended to unplug only to have a nervous breakdown because we had the fear of missing out. That fear now has its own acronym, FOMO. When was the last time you've seen anyone without their phone in hand? We now carry in only one bag of groceries at a time because we're holding our phone. We can't hold our kids without fumbling with our phone. We don't shake hands because we are holding our phone. Why? Why do we succumb to this pressure? Why has instant gratification at all costs become the norm? Why are we frantic to get the story, to be selected, to be heard?

I believe the answer is because we are scared. We're uncertain what tomorrow will look like. We aren't sure if we'll be downsized. We want to be the best, be the smartest, and to be the go-to person. We're afraid of not being noticed or valued. We are anxious to get our needs met.

This is the reality we are living in. The result is at a personal cost: higher stress, health issues (heart disease, diabetes, mental health), addictions (drugs, food, exercise, shopping), and broken relationships (divorce, estrangement, detachments). We push ourselves to the brink in order to avoid these things only to become these things because we are pushing ourselves.

But it doesn't have to be this way. People do not need to continue on this hamster wheel. You can get ahead, have a healthy life, and reach fulfillment, while still reaching full potential as a person and as an organization. You can be the executive who thrives without paying a life-threatening price. You can be the manager who goes on vacation and leaves your phone in your hotel room while you're at the beach. You can be the employee who truly knows what work/life balance really means. It starts with looking within. It starts with understanding just where you are at on the influence spectrum.

Leaders, executives, and managers find themselves in all sorts of situations. Do you trust your gut or listen to advisors moving in the opposite direction? How do you recognize what is in your blindspot? What is the best way to inspire true engagement based on curiosity and not just lip service? How do you separate ego from action? These are questions that every leader faces during their tenure. The answers lie in becoming and being influential. It's time to trust your confidence to guide you. Express your passion to motivate others. Invest in being likeable and trustworthy with everyone you meet.

There are five competencies that organizations look for in their employees, no matter where they are in the company: leadership, communication, team effectiveness, strategy/solutions, and execution/evaluation. Every person within an organization is a communicator, leader, team member, strategist, and executor. Do you see yourself in those roles? Do you see how these influence traits interweave with everything? Let's see.

Impact of Confidence on Leadership

Julie was a rising star in the organization. She asked the right questions and wasn't afraid to stretch herself. Julie was a high performer which opened the door for several promotions. Until this one. Julie was promoted to an executive leadership position in the marketing department. She suddenly found herself having to live up to a whole new set of expectations and performance standards. People were coming at her from all directions. Julie was experiencing more pressure than she ever had before. In the usual Julie form, she tackled things head on. But the results weren't what she was used to. Sometimes projects didn't meet the deadline. Other times, direct reports didn't fulfill their responsibilities and she had to cover for them. Everything was at a faster pace, with higher stakes. She was playing in the big league now.

After about three months, things began to fall apart. Managing time, fearing failure, and feeling overwhelmed were constantly on Julie's mind. This started to affect her contributions during team meetings and planning. Because of her limiting belief that if she was seen as struggling she would get fired, she began to withdraw. She stopped returning phone calls, backed away from challenging situations, and was reluctant to take risks. Julie feared losing respect from peers and disappointing the decision makers who believed in her future at the firm. This all took its toll on Julie. The stress she felt was causing frustration and a feeling of insecurity.

In a word, Julie got derailed. She still had the same skills and talent but something changed. The root cause was an acute loss of confidence. Self-doubt begin to set in. Julie began questioning if she was really qualified to be in her position. Maybe it took more than hard work? Maybe her skills needed to be refined better? Maybe she didn't have what it took to be a leader? Julie took these concerns to her mentor at the company. Soon Julie began working with an executive coach who helped her address her confidence issues. By investing in Julie, the company knew they were supporting one of their best emerging leaders. They made a commitment to identify the problem and solve it by working with her, a hallmark of an influential organization. Eventually, Julie understood the connection between her confidence and her performance. She regained her faith in herself, and went on to become an influential leader.

Organizations win when they create influential leaders.

Leaders are tasked with getting results, from building profits and increasing productivity to increasing efficiencies and inspiring innovation. Every single person in the organization plays a part in leading these efforts.

Impact of Trustworthiness on Communication

The story is told of a country store owner who saw his young clerk at the front counter talking to a customer. The owner was horrified as he heard the young man tell the woman, "No, ma'am we don't have any of that and looks like we won't for quite a while."

The store owner ran to the front frantically and blurted out, "Yes, we have it on order, and it'll be here next week. Don't you worry about it."

As soon as the woman left, the owner reprimanded the clerk. "Don't you EVER tell a customer that again! You have to cover up the fact that we are out of it with the statement that it's on its way, even if you know it's not on order.

"Yes sir," dutifully responded the young clerk.
"By the way, what was she wanting?" asked the store owner.
"Rain," replied the clerk.

Telling a small or large lie has become second nature in many organizations. We are sometimes encouraged by our superiors or co-workers to stretch the truth. While lying or "maneuvering the truth" may serve to offer a short-term relief, it ultimately breaks long-term trust and lessens our ability to communicate effectively, which is ultimately more problematic than a short-term problem fix. Lowering our trustworthiness lowers our integrity AND our ability to influence and be influential.

We don't often see that we are lying because we simply skirt the truth. Employees find themselves in predicaments like this all too often. For example, Kyle was tasked with giving an exact overview of inventory during the acquisition of his company. The deal was in the making and crucial to the company's survival. However, Kyle was faced with a dilemma. His boss directed him to not include new pricing, hence, hiding actual inventory expenses. Kyle didn't want to lie. He believed it was wrong to "cover up" this information. But Kyle also needed his job. He had responsibilities and a family who depended on him. Over the next few weeks, Kyle began experiencing sleepless nights, frustration at home with his family, and not wanting to come to work. He began missing work and eventually started looking for a new job. The company lost a great employee when Kyle took his conscience and quit.

Life may not be black and white, but trust should never be a gray area. The main reason people become untrustworthy comes down to a single word: fear. Fear is one of, if not the, most powerful motivators. Lying is typically a flight mechanism attached to fear. We don't like what is presenting itself, and so we attempt to manipulate the truth for our own protection or gain. It effects how we communicate to and with each other.

Once this behavior and breakdown occurs, people become afraid of negative consequences (loss of position, prestige, job or simply loss of face). They are afraid of losing the illusion they've created for others. People lie because they are afraid they won't get what they want or they will lose control over the situation. All of these situations involve fear. And they all lead to the person not being seen as trustworthy.

How Does Trust Impact Communication?

A lack of trust creates distance between people, and lends itself to being misunderstood, building walls, extinguishing loyalty, removing expectations, loss of diverse ideas and points of view, feeds ill-thwarted intentions, and eventually truth becomes a misnomer in the organization.

When we fail to be truth-tellers and trustworthy, our communication becomes inauthentic and ineffective. We lose connections to each other. Hidden agendas erupt. Employee morale, overall innovation and efficiency suffers. The life blood – communication – of the organization is cut short. Are we being influential here? Absolutely not.

Impact of Commitment on Team Effectiveness

After eighteen years in operations with a major global IT company, Debra was finally promoted to the executive suite. She was the recognized expert – realizing extensive success for the company. Debra now thought she had her chance to effect more change company wide. This promotion also brought with it being part of the executive team where all executives congregated to exchange views and promote specific change efforts in the company.

After the first three months of meetings, Debra realized that these meetings basically were gossip sessions. Many of the executives aired their dirty laundry, complained about their departments and criticized people in the C-Suite. Debra was appalled. She had no idea that these people, whom she knew independently, were like this behind closed doors. Debra found herself in a dilemma. The team wasn't practicing best practices nor were they accomplishing the objective of this executive team. The work wasn't getting done. Now she realized why people in middle management were frustrated. The impact this team had was detrimental to all systems that answered to it. Debra's excitement of participating in the executive suite was now greatly diminished. She began to wonder how she could affect any change within this team. Debra began to see each team meeting as a never-ending exercise in convincing herself to show up. She even began promising herself rewards like a small online shopping spree or a cupcake if she did. Debra lost interest, and eventually just put her time in. The biggest barrier to effective teams is commitment. Debra certainly lost hers.

The Biggest Barrier To Effective Teams Is Lack of Commitment.

Teams are successful when its members share the desire (and commitment) to achieve success through high levels of participation and collaboration. This level of success depends not so much on the content of the team, although it is critical to achieve the task, but success depends on the team's ability to commit to the process. Process is not what is said, but *how* it is said. Team process is the method or the way the team functions regardless of the goal. It is important that each team member inspire the commitment of other members to participate in the process of the team. How does a team member inspire commitment? You guessed it. By being influential.

Impact of Courage on Strategy

Some people are naturally tuned in to organizational strategy, but being a strategist has its challenges. There is relentless pressure for greater profits, increased complexity of expectations, and dealing with unmotivated managers who are only allowed low levels of involvement in the process. Everyone is part of the company strategy regardless if you were sitting at the table in the wee hours of the night developing it.

Let's take a look at Ben. His company invested heavily in sending Ben to numerous training seminars on the art of strategy and strategic planning. Ben was eager to learn and had a certain knack and talent for seeing what could be in the future. He was drawn to how a company could find bigger and better solutions to current problems and even problems that didn't yet exist. Then the unthinkable happened. Because of downsizing demands, a new executive was assigned to oversee Ben's department, and Ben was now to work with a peer who really didn't have the first clue about strategy.

This changed Ben's entire strategic planning landscape

from one of freedom to explore, test, and challenge to constantly looking over his shoulder and worrying about new ideas being shot down without consideration. All of a sudden, Ben found himself drowning under an executive who had no appreciation for what it took to think strategically or innovate solutions for potential problems. And to top it off, he now had to contend with a co-worker who was draining all his energy.

Ben began to question whether he was any good at it anymore. He started to believe that maybe his creativity had run its course. Ben wondered that strategy may not be his forte and maybe he needed to do something different, go someplace different.

Another wasted employee. Ben's company didn't pay attention to what was happening right under their nose. This situation could have played out differently if the organization had invested in developing Ben's courage along with his strategic prowess.

Strategy is the foundation used by companies to make the most of its valuable resources. It is the connective tissue between layers of management and between functions. Strategy provides the lens helping us stay focused and not be distracted by an ever-changing environment. This definition of strategy takes courage. It takes fortitude to challenge old ways of thinking, to stay present in a changing world and tackle issues as they arise, even if those issues are the making of the company itself.

What makes the difference? Being influential. An influential strategist creates lasting value over time, without sacrificing financial performance. An influential strategist brings all stakeholders and markets together to create the transformations necessary to thrive. The ability to produce great strategy is more than processes, methodologies, data analysis, and capabilities; although important, these are not the driving force behind an influential strategist. What really differentiates an influential strategist is courage.

Courage Is What Really Differentiates An Influential Strategist.

From the above example, Ben didn't have the courage to confront what was happening. He believed that if he were to confront the situation, he'd be criticized for not being a team player or falling into step with the new landscape of the company. Ben found himself backing away from problems instead of looking forward to solving them.

Courage is the strength or determination to meet daunting circumstances head-on. It is called upon when action is needed, when the future looks hard, scary, or risky. In the context of business strategy, it's the preparedness to have difficult conversations, to inspire courageous ideas, and to make courageous choices or, in Ben's case, to act courageously.

Enhancing executive commitment relies on purposeful conversations that are deliberate and central to the obvious. It takes courage to initiate these conversations, to not only ask questions, but to question the answers to those questions. This is critical especially during a time of immense disruption and uncertainty, aka downsizing.

To accomplish this level of strategy, the influential strategist is comfortable with the uncomfortable, confronts uncertainty, and challenges long-standing convention. It takes courage to challenge traditional business assumptions and make choices that dictate a drastic change in direction. The courageous influential strategist thinks broadly in how the business or market environment will be different in three, five or ten years. Often this means balancing underestimating the risk of the status quo while overestimating the risk of doing something new or different.

This is how courage differentiates the influential strategist. Being influential and being courageous are skills that can be learned.

Impact of Empowering and Likeability on Execution

It was David's job to execute the operations piece of a pharmaceutical company's strategic plan. He was doing his best to stay focused, but his frustration with the group was growing. He had no idea of how to hold people accountable. Instead he would blow up when people missed their mark, especially when it all fell apart at the last minute. The group said they completed each assignment, so they were confused why David was frustrated with them. This was a repeated cycle every time the stakes were high. David needed to reach a performance level where his team would deliver or execute the expected outcomes. This affected how David felt about his work, and eventually, his overall passion for company goals.

When David brought this issue to his coaching sessions, we began to uncover long held beliefs and behaviors that were hurting David rather than helping him be a better executor of plans. For example, David would give orders to the group specifying what needed to be done by when. Throughout that timeline, David realized that he was constantly checking up on people. What he didn't realize was that he was in reality micromanaging them. Fear was driving David's behavior to get perfect results. David was so focused on getting results that he didn't take any time to uncover any hidden talents within the group. He didn't stop to consider what they could contribute or how others would make his life better by assuming not only responsibly but freedom to implement better ideas to get results. He had tunnel vision.

David didn't share information. He thought people wouldn't know what to do with it. Besides, he believed he was the only one who was smart enough to make things happen. David recognized that he was so consumed with day-to-day activities that he basically ignored the group's needs to contribute, to make mistakes, to find success, or to be trusted. After several months of coaching, David realized that he was responsible for his own frustration. He hadn't empowered his people. Because of his actions and attitude, these people didn't find him approachable, caring or likeable. Thus they stopped supporting him and took little ownership for the execution of plans.

Successful Execution Means Earning The Trust And Respect Of People On Your Team.

Understanding that people need the freedom to experiment, make mistakes and step outside their comfort zone to be as creative or innovative as they can be, is when you will reach greater accomplishment than you thought possible. When people experience you this way, they will meet head-on unexpected problems that need solutions. They will exercise flexibility when plans change. And they will give you their best because they have made a commitment to you because you have empowered them to do so. It is all possible. It simply takes understanding what is needed to improve one's ability to truly be influential.

The bottom line is this. Being influential carries the day no matter what area or position a person works: leadership, communication, teams, strategy, or execution. Every person functions at some level in each of these areas. These competencies aren't assigned only to one person or one per person. Everyone is a leader. Everyone communicates. Everyone is part of a team. Everyone buys into the strategy. And everyone plays their part in the execution of the company mission. These core competencies make or break a company's future level of success. How to improve these competencies? Taking the plunge into the waters of influence and mastering what it means to really be influential. The difference means better leadership, better communication, better teams, better strategy, and better execution. Are you game?

Chapter Ten Checklist

- ☐ When there's an elephant in the room, introduce him. Shake his hand.

- ☐ Be happy to have FOMO – you really aren't missing much.

- ☐ Organizations win when they create influential leaders.

- ☐ Never a good idea to skirt the truth.

- ☐ Trust is never a gray area.

- ☐ Fear is a powerful motivator. How is it motivating you?

- ☐ The lifeblood of an organization is communication.

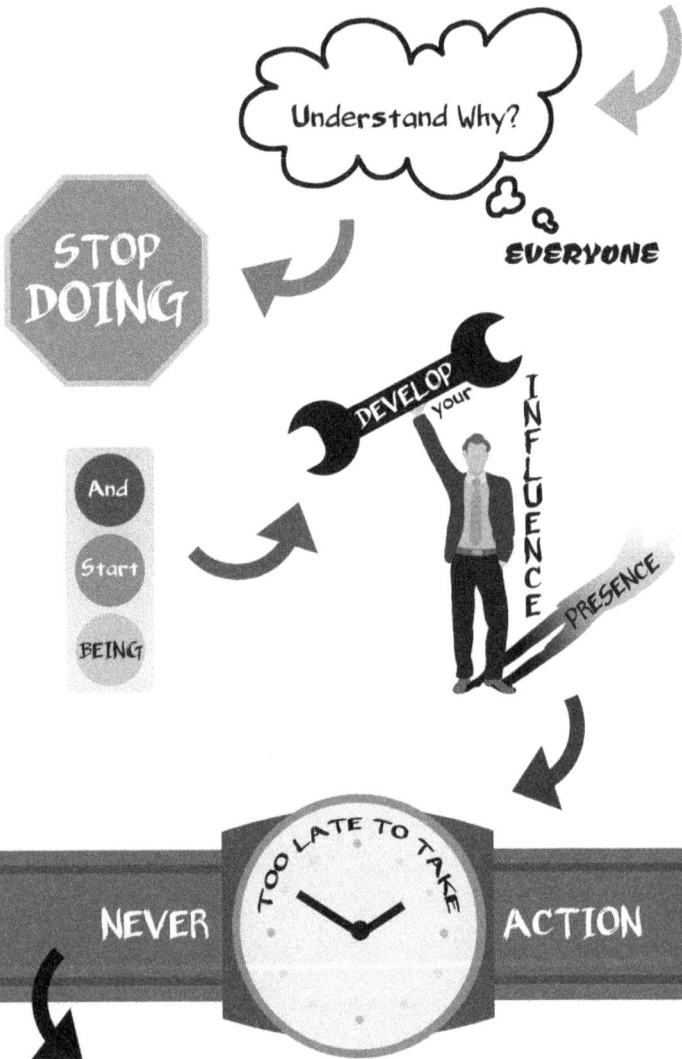

Build Your Influence Potential

Example is not the main thing in influencing others, it's the only thing.

- ALBERT SCHWEITZER

B usiness is about people, and people are about human nature, and the problems we experience professionally and personally are common to us all. The root cause of any organization's problems or victories is due to the impact or actions we have with each other as people. That is what being influential means and that is why the Keller Influence Indicator® (KII®) was created. Influence is the "make or break" factor and we have not been fully in tune with how being influential is not the same as having influence AND that we all can learn how to become influential. We can stop DOING and begin BEING. By understanding the traits that affect being influential, the fact that we all possess these traits, and that we all can master them is the paradigm shift that takes a person and an organization to unprecedented levels of success.

Stop DOING and Start BEING

You have complete control over your Seven Influence Traits®. You build your likability. You find your passion. You cement your commitment. You generate your trustworthiness. You use these traits in every facet of your life, whether you're

- Having a difficult conversation in the board room
- Managed by a supervisor you do not like or who micromanages
- Working with a boss that absolutely loves your ideas
- Working on a promotion and advancement
- Needing to manage up
- Working with people who covet other people's ideas

Without knowing it, you are using your Seven Influence Traits® in every conversation you have.

When was the last time you talked to someone about your ability to empower others? Or your desire to be more likeable? I'm guessing not a lot. However, when was the last time someone said you're a control freak? Or you don't listen very well? You see, its behavior that gets all the attention. Organizations and people **STOP THERE.** That's the big mistake. To be a leader in your industry, once you identify the behavior, it is critical to look beyond the obvious. You need to ask, "What is the reason or the cause of this behavior?" Instead, people make incorrect assumptions, and wrong conclusions, based only on what they see.

It is in the best interest of EVERYONE to seek to understand why.

Do not give people false hope by employing tips and tricks for change. Remember, instead of giving a man a fish, teach him how to fish. Instead of giving a person a cheat sheet of what to do, teach him or her how to be. My mission is to help organizations *teach their people how to fish,* how to develop themselves to be the best employees they can be. The way to achieve the highest degree of influence, trust, and engagement is developing people through the lens of being influential. People need to know that they can course correct when they are deficient in a particular trait, and get what they want and need. Once this happens, people will contribute more and feel good about doing so.

What will it mean to you (and your organization) once you begin to live and experience your Seven Influence Traits®? How will it affect your career and your future? How will courage help you in having a difficult conversation? What role will likeability play when you are confronted with a challenge at work? How will growing your confidence, building your trustworthiness, or expressing more passion serve you? These are the questions that should resonate with you.

To understand the relevance and application of the Seven Influence Traits®, ask yourself these two questions:

1. What would happen in my organization if confidence was removed from everyone in my company?

2. How would my company look if trustworthiness was raised by 25 percent in every employee from the top to the bottom?

In addition to wanting to have great abundance of all seven traits, to really embrace the idea or concept of being influential by building these traits is to understand the ramifications of losing any one of these traits as well. The things we take for granted are often things that need to be addressed in a new light.

Common sense tells us that when a person's confidence is high, they think better about themselves, take more risks, build better relationships, and reach peak performance on the job. Common sense also tells us that when a person's confidence is low, they lose faith in their abilities, subscribe to self-limiting beliefs, and they underachieve.

When a person's ability to empower is high, brilliant ideas come forth, learning spikes, and untapped resources are shared. When a person's ability to empower is low, creativity is blocked, engagement gets short-circuited, and morale plummets.

Becoming Your Best Self

The Keller Influence Indicator® (KII®) is a statistically validated tool that accurately measures how well developed or positioned a person's Seven Influence Traits® are.

The KII® can provide enormous insight that is useful in discovering who you are but also who you've learned to be. Too often people become what others expect them to be. When this happens there is tremendous pressure to conform and not be authentic. So what happens when a person becomes someone other than who they are? They become disconnected from what they want and begin to feel empty and unmotivated. Relationships suffer. Self-esteem suffers. Work suffers.

During the launch of the KII® I listened to client feedback about their experience with the assessment. (I still do.) I heard everything from one senior executive in the media industry ask me if I had spoken to his mother (accuracy of the reports) to "Wow – I'm ready to dig in and improve NOW!" But one story in particular stood out.

Someone in the publishing industry, we'll call him Jack, who had risen to great heights in his career as evidenced by numerous awards and global recognition. Jack found the KII® interesting so he took the assessment and the results astounded him. And me. Jack's influence trait scores were much lower than I/he would have anticipated given his status and success.

I looked into why his scores came out this way. During our consultation, (after I got over being star-struck), Jack said he wasn't able to sleep after seeing his results. He was puzzled and concerned. We looked into the individual items on the assessment. Jack had answered half of the KII® items dedicated to each specific trait in one direction, and the other half in the opposite direction. In other words, I explained to him that he was in great conflict with himself. Half of the items represented who he was and the other half represented who he had learned to be.

There was a long emotional silence. Then Jack said, "That explains why I lost my family." He went on to recollect how, in his industry, it was a cutthroat dog-eat-dog business. He did what he needed to do to get ahead and make it to the top. He confessed he didn't even recognize himself.

I shared with him that there was good news. The person that he was, who he liked, who was genuine, and who made good choices, still existed. Jack's relief was palpable. After a few more coaching conversations, Jack is now moving in the direction of returning to who he really is. He is even promoting a different mindset in his industry.

That's why this assessment tool is so valuable. You see where you are at with each trait and then are given the tools to improve and master each trait. Being yourself, your true self and becoming your best self is the key. It's so much easier being who you are than always having to remember what to do. Why? Because who you are, deep inside, your very nature, is the genesis of all your actions.

This is powerful stuff. Looking at your own level of confidence, commitment, or trustworthiness is not for the faint of heart. The KII® is for organizations and people who want to seriously understand how they can be happier, contribute more, be part of an influential culture, and create businesses that prosper.

Benefits of Mastering Your Ability To Be Influential

Mastering your ability to be influential involves (for you and the organization):

- Increasing confidence in your skills – know what you know and do it well – continue developing
- Staying committed to your professional development – life-long learning – never stop asking where do I need to improve?

- Courageously asking tough questions – not being afraid to ask what is tough to answer
- Empowering your vulnerability to explore – set the stage to uncover what needs to exist for you to contribute to the company goal
- Expanding your trustworthiness so people will trust your intentions – this is foundational in all relationships
- Passionately walking your talk – be a solid role model with your own traits
- Being likeable opens doors to potential long-term healthy work and personal relationships – the first stage of being productive

Never Too Late To Take Action

The time has come for organizations to understand the needs of emerging leaders, millennials, and an overall changing workforce. You need to understand what is at the heart of all business and at the heart of all happiness. The question is: *are you ready?*

Do you have the best people in the right places to actually carry out your mission? Are they confident, courageous, and passionate? Will they be able to make the necessary commitment especially when the pressure is on or conflict runs the day? Have you done everything you can to be competitive, to deliver on your promises, all the while keeping and growing great talent?

People need help to be the best they can be, to perform with all cylinders firing. They need to know how influential they are. They need to know how to build their influence in a way that will have long returns. They need to know how to effectively use their influence.

Influence Presence

Being influential, rather than just influencing, represents the single most valuable aspect of your character that inspires how people respond to you. When you are trustworthy, people will trust you. When you are courageous, people will stop and listen. When you are passionate, people will cheer for you. These responses show up based on your intentions. Are they honorable? Are they for the good of the company, the community, or society? Will they lead to better opportunities? Will your intentions support making a difference?

It doesn't matter if you are answering the phones, constructing the strategic plan, or coaching high potential performers. What does matter is that you are aware of your presence in doing all of the above. Presence is a prerequisite for being influential whether you're an artist, a thoracic surgeon, or an administrative assistant.

What is it about a person that allows them to command a room with so little (seemingly) effort? What is it they have that other people don't? It's their presence. And strong presence influences everyone and everything.

Presence can be a pattern of behavior, plenty of eye contact, an exuding energy, or even poised silence. It can be many things. But the one thing all aspects of presence have in common is how proficient a person is in their Seven Influence Traits®. Presence originates from how you feel about yourself–it's an internal process. When you believe yourself to be worthy, capable, and competent, people respond to you as worthy, capable, and competent.

Although I have not had the privilege of meeting the Dalai Lama in person, I've heard it said that hearing him speak was like being the in the presence of God. The feeling of peace that comes over a person is life-changing. It is said he has a laugh that can melt hearts and open minds. This image of the Dalai Lama reinforces his famous quote, "To change the world, we must first change ourselves." The Dalai Lama carries a small bag with him. In this bag are several pieces of candy, extra reading glasses, an under-arm thermometer, and a toothbrush kit, because he believes it is important to brush after every meal.

The Dalai Lama has stated, "Everyone needs a strong sense of self. Without it, you are weak. It is from this sense of self that compassion, determination and altruism are born."

The Dalai Lama has presence. The way to create a strong presence begins by believing that people like you, which in turn causes you to behave likeable. In the beginning, you can simply imagine that they like you and act accordingly. Another way to develop strong presence is to know you belong. This helps you become comfortable in your space. Ignore self-doubt. Stop second guessing yourself. Expect to be acknowledged. Lastly, to have strong presence you need to realize we are all in the same boat. Every person has the innate need to contribute, be productive, and give and receive love (something I learned from a man who suffered from schizophrenia).

Believing you are loved, acting like you belong, and realizing you are not much different than anyone else, happens from being who you are–a confident person who courageously makes a commitment to what you passionately believe in. That feels like an influential person, does it not? It is absolutely possible for you.

Chapter Eleven Checklist

- ☐ Business is about people, and people are about human nature.

- ☐ The biggest barrier to effective teams is commitment.

- ☐ Stop DOING and start BEING.

- ☐ It is in everyone's best interest to seek to understand why.

- ☐ Master your ability to be influential. It's a journey not a race.

- ☐ It's never too late to start. In fact, now is the best time.

- ☐ Strong presence allows you to command the room.

The Power of Focus

Knowing and Building Influence Can:

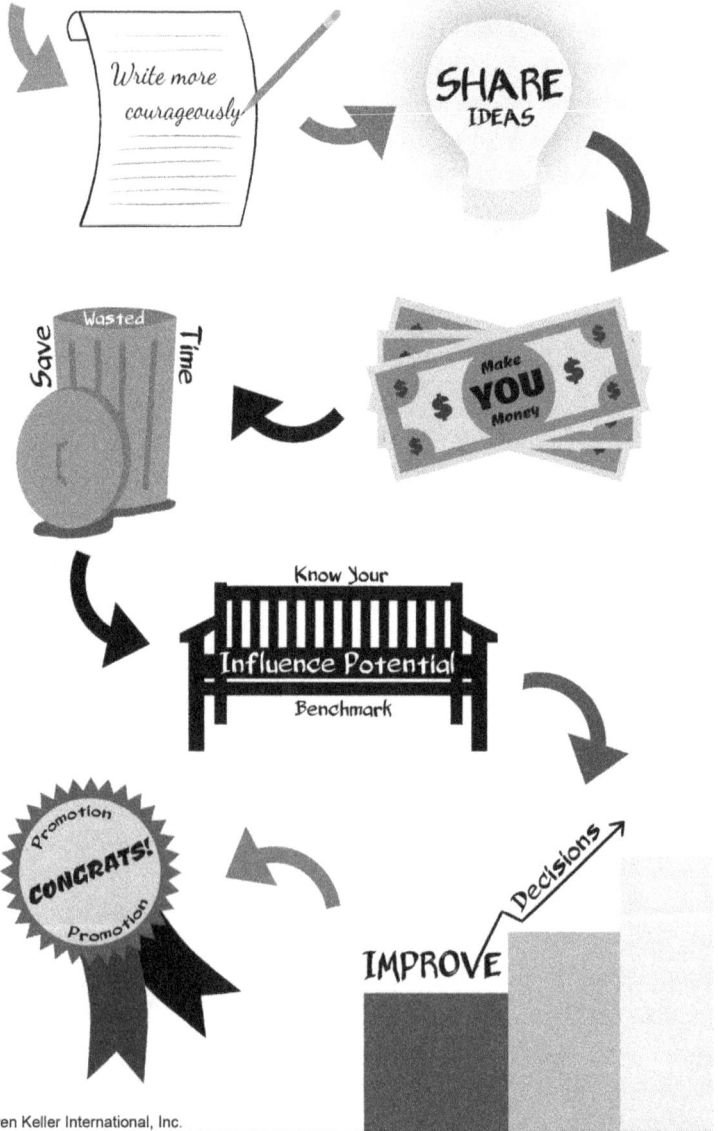

Write more courageously

SHARE IDEAS

Save Wasted Time

Make YOU Money

Know Your
Influence Potential
Benchmark

Promotion
CONGRATS!
Promotion

IMPROVE Decisions

The Power of Focus

*Any intelligent fool can make things
bigger and more complex. It takes a
touch of genius – and a lot of courage –
to move in the opposite direction.*

- ALBERT EINSTEIN

Marie Curie was the first woman to win a Nobel Prize and the first person and only woman to win the award in two different fields (physics and chemistry). Marie was born in Warsaw, Poland during the control of the czar of Russia. Before Marie was 11, her sister had died of typhus and her mother had died of tuberculosis. At age 15, Marie left Poland and traveled to France where she worked as a governess for seven years, before beginning her own studies. Marie Curie, along with her husband Pierre, developed the theory of radioactivity. Marie Curie had a defined sense of purpose so strong that she overcame insurmountable odds to achieve. Her work forced the reconsideration of the foundation of physics. She knew the power of focus and commitment.

Most of us never really grasp the power of focus. There

are so many distractions and demands especially as we live in a global age. And because of technology we are privy to everything that goes on everywhere. No wonder we can't focus! Ah yes, we give lip service to focus: I'll lose 10 pounds, I'll learn to communication better, I'll improve my listening, and the list goes on. But what is at the heart of focus? What is it that sets those who really focus (and achieve) apart from those who *think* they're focusing?

Author Remez Sasson shares a story of a teacher and his student walking from one village to another when they suddenly heard a roar of a tiger behind them. "What shall we do, Master?" asked the student.

The teacher answered in a calm voice: "There are several options. We can fill our minds with paralyzing fear so that we cannot move, and let the tiger do with us whatever pleases it. We can faint. We can run away, but then it will run after us. We can fight with it, but physically it is stronger than us. We can pray to God to save us. We can choose to influence the tiger with the power of our mind, if our concentration is strong enough. We can send it love. We can also concentrate and meditate on our inner power, and on the fact that we are one with the entire universe, including the tiger, and in this way influence its soul. Which option do you choose?"

"You are the Master. You tell me what to do. We don't have much time," the student responded.

The master turned his gaze fearlessly towards the tiger, emptied his mind from all thoughts, and entered a deep state of meditation. In his consciousness, he embraced everything in the universe, including the tiger. In this state the consciousness of the teacher became one with consciousness of the tiger.

Meanwhile the student started to shiver with fear, as the tiger was quite close, ready to make a leap at them. He was amazed at how his teacher could stay so calm and detached in the face of danger.

The teacher continued to meditate without fear. After a little while, the tiger gradually lowered its head and tail and went away. The student asked his teacher in astonishment, "What did you do?"

"I cleared all thoughts from my mind and united myself in spirit with the tiger. We became united in peace on the spiritual level. The tiger sensed the inner calmness, peace, and unity and felt no threat or need to express violence, and so walked away. When the mind is silent and calm, its peace is automatically transmitted to everything and everyone around, influencing them deeply," concluded the teacher.

When you operate from a calm core of mastery of your Seven Influence Traits® you influence everyone around you. Influential people know that focus is a key ingredient to success. They understand that in order to accomplish what they want, they need to focus. They also know that it takes discipline. To attain that level of discipline requires a person to make a personal commitment to what they want – a commitment so strong that nothing will deter them from their goal. So success depends on focus, focus requires discipline, and discipline is a result of commitment.

Think of it this way, you want to be noticed as a future leader at work. You know you have to build trust in order to be considered. You realize that building trust is a time consuming ordeal that means being reliable, keeping promises, accepting responsibility, and showing a willingness to help. Wow, getting noticed as a leader has just gotten harder. Where will you begin? Do you decide this is too much work? Are you willing to do what it takes to become a trustworthy person?

The person who will get noticed as the next company leader is the person who makes a commitment where nothing will stand in their way to get there. Be prepared that it will take time, you will have setbacks, and there will be days that you will want to throw in the towel. That is why you need to grow your commitment muscles. Commitment represents a defined sense of purpose. Once that purpose is identified, you are dedicated to it through your intention and action of furthering growth, learning and promise – the promise to yourself.

My life's work is all about personal growth and I just might own every self-help book ever published. They sit on the shelf next to all the business methodology books, which is the shelf below every business and leadership biography. I've amassed my own library (and spent a small fortune in literature). I love being able to eavesdrop into how some of our greatest leaders and most successful business people did things. Yet although these books are valuable and useful, and I learned a lot from them, they didn't tell me about me. That, I realized, **was the missing piece.** How was I doing? Where did I need to start? Which concept or quality did I need to possess more of to reach where these successful people performed at?

I believe the best ideas come from solving common problems and that query for me became: What could we accomplish if we knew more about our own potential for success, for leadership, for impacting others? With that in mind, it became important to me that people, while knowing all the great information that fill our libraries and book stores, had a way to understand themselves better in relation to all that great information. I created a way with my assessment tool that people could have the insight into what it was about them that they needed to grow, build, or change in order to achieve beyond what they thought possible. All of the learning and research became deeply personal, where it truly matters.

I set out to learn and know as much as I could about each trait, how we used them, why we needed them, the role they played in our growth, why people dismissed them, basically everything about their existence! Over the course of 20-plus years, I've coached hundreds, if not thousands, of people: CEOs, senior executives, board members, managers and supervisors, teams, and entrepreneurs. It all comes down to people and how we relate to each other.

Dale Carnegie, in **"How to Win Friends and Influence People"** stated, "About 15 percent of one's financial success is due to one's technical knowledge and about 85 percent is due to skill in human engineering – to personality and the ability to lead people." Leading people is all about influence.

My father was right. I am my best asset. He taught me that what I put in my brain is important and needed, but what I carry in my heart and my soul matters more. That is how people will see me, that is how people will experience me, that is how people will respond to me, and that is how people will remember me. My parents showed me how to step forward and be aware that not only what I do but who I am has greater impact on everyone around me.

With this upbringing in hand, having coached more than twenty years, in all different time zones, from the team room to the board room, I decided to follow my passion of helping people build their influence. That was at the core of my coaching. I didn't subscribe to the traditional models or concepts of persuasion, subtle manipulation, or negotiation. I coach at a deeper level.

Influence as generally taught is based on the outward or external piece: If I say or do this, then you will say or do that. I knew something was missing. My question was, "What do I need to bring to the table in order to influence someone?" In other words, who does a person need to be in order to impact another's life or even their own? There's a fundamental internal occurrence that needs to take place before anyone can successfully and with integrity impact another life. This is when I developed the concept behind being influential.

Being Influential Is More Than Just Telling Someone What To Do

As you now see, there is a difference between influencing and being influential. The greatest figures in history and the great philosophers had something more about them that made them highly influential. Something that made people stop and listen and follow of their own free will and desire. These people possessed something that caused others to ask questions, to entertain new ideas, and break away from limiting thoughts that didn't serve them well. People were drawn to their message.

What made these people effective wasn't what they did, but who they were. The most influential people had an abundance of the qualities that I now label the Seven Influence Traits®: confidence, commitment, courage, passion, empowering, trustworthiness, and likeability.

The potential of being influential exists for every human being on this planet. Every person has these Seven

Influence Traits®. The difference between someone who is influential and the person who isn't lies in how well a person maximizes each and every trait. The person who nurtures and embraces each of these traits in abundance exhibits great influence – because they are first influential.

We've all failed or been rejected. The influential person uses their courage to start over, or their commitment that drives them to find another way, or their confidence to understand what went wrong. It doesn't matter where you come from or the experiences you have. Everyone has the choice to be better, to make a difference, and show up as influential as you can be.

These traits are used at work, at home, in your community. They are at play in all your relationships. Being influential isn't something you take in and out of a box. Being influential shows up everywhere, in a process, a person, a pattern of behavior. Being influential shows up in your body language, tone, words, and actions. The question becomes, how are you building and maximizing your influence potential - these Seven Influence Traits®?

You can start immediately to influence yourself. Tomorrow morning when you wake up, before you reach over to turn the alarm off, or put your feet on the floor, do this first. Smile. You don't need a reason. Just smile. You don't need to think about something that will make you smile. All you need to do is smile. If it doesn't happen, take your two fingers and push up on your cheeks so that your lips go up and you are smiling. I guarantee you will experience something. There will be impact. See how this one act influences the rest of your day. For many people this takes courage. It takes a commitment to take charge of how your day will begin.

The act of smiling is a neuro-chemical change that occurs in the brain when your lips are in the shape of a smile. When I put a smile on my face, my mind begins to entertain something enjoyable or fun. My mind reminds me to be grateful. I think about the blessings I have in my life. Just by doing that one thing, putting a smile on your face, every single morning, can determine how your day will go. How you choose to influence or impact yourself is very powerful. And this is just one small example.

I've never met anyone who didn't think being influential was important. That is why I take such pleasure in my work and the KII®. This assessment gives you, and your organization, what has been missing – the benchmark of your own influence potential. Now you can know where you are starting from. It's like taking a test for blood sugar. Don't tell me that I might have high blood sugar. Tell me if I do. Tell me what the number is so I know where to start, what I have to do to get it in check. Being influential is the same way. Once you know where you are, then and only then, is when you can move forward, putting into place the necessary beliefs and behaviors to be influential.

It's like building a house. In order to have a solid steady house you need a sound foundation. If the foundation has cracks, the house will eventually crumble. People and organizations are no different. When we fail to build a solid foundation, one of being influential, what we go on to build eventually crumbles, too.

What is the Keller Influence Indicator® (KII®)?

A Valid and Reliable Measurement of Potential – Only one of its kind in the world. It is scientifically validated and reliable. It measures influence potential.

A Benchmark or Baseline – Shows an individual's score on each particular trait. That score represents where you currently are at that point in time with regard to that specific trait.

A Reference for Knowing Where to Start – Scores point exactly where a person is on each trait and provides a starting position for knowing what to do to improve.

A Shortcut to Understanding Why – Answers the questions about what strengths and challenges the client is facing in accomplishing their goals.

A Way to Track Progress over Time – Re-test is available for clients after coaching to strengthen and increase traits. Progress is noticed at face value through goal achievement, fulfillment, and overall life satisfaction.

Used for Leadership and Sales Development/ Problem Solving – Foundation for achieving great success in leading people, teams and organizations.

What the KII® is not: A Personality Test; an Attitudes Measurement; an EQ (Emotional Intelligence) Measurement; a Competency Profile. The KII® measures characteristics - the Seven Influence Traits® - that are significant for personal and professional success. This tool is not for sissies. It takes concerted effort, desire and a willingness to understand the fundamentals and competencies of each influence trait and to master them.

If you are looking for a quick fix, this is not the process to pursue. Building an influential culture is a marathon, not a sprint.

Here's what knowing and building your influence potential can do for you:
- Speak more courageously (self-expression is critical for influence)
- Share your ideas confidently to the team (this is where tomorrow innovations originate from)
- Save you wasted time (from obsessing, self-doubting)
- Get access to more information
- Become the go-to person in a crunch (because your advice is extremely valuable)
- Make you a great deal of money
- Set you up to be a better (and highly effective) communicator
- Improve your decisions
- Receive the promotion you deserve
- Make people want to help (follow, listen to) you
- And much more . . .

Here's how you can begin building your influence potential and an influence culture in your organization:

1. Take the pulse of your organization or company.
Ask these questions.
a. What is no longer working?
b. How have our people changed?
c. What needs are not being met? Organizational and personal.
d. Are we helping people access their potential?

    e. What does our partnership look like with our employees?

2. Review the culture dynamics.
    a. What are the stories of the organization?
    b. What are the unspoken rules?
    c. Know what shapes your culture.
        i. Assumptions
        ii. Values
        iii. Beliefs
        iv. Expectation
        v. Patterns of behavior

3. Measure the Influence Potential of your people.
(www.Karen-Keller.com)
    a. Identify High Potentials.
    b. Identify emerging leaders.
    c. Build and inspire management.
    d. Match the right person to the right job.
    e. Predict individual and team success.
    f. Discover how people show up as:
        i. Leaders
        ii. Communicators
        iii. Team members
        iv. Strategists
        v. Executors
    g. Assess strengths and challenges.
    h. Measure the Seven Influence Traits[®] (benchmark).

4. Set people up for success.
    a. How are you making people successful?

b. How are people taking ownership for their success?

c. How are you building influential teams?

That truly is the heart and soul of the KII® - to set you (and your organization) up for success. I work with clients to enhance and maximize these seven traits. The results are astounding and that makes my work so rewarding.

One never knows what influence or impact they will have on another person either immediately or years later. For example, think of the teacher who turned you onto a certain passion that is now your life's work, or a friend who stopped you from making a terrible decision or a mentor at work who showed what true leadership looks like. We all have been on the receiving end of influence and we all have opportunities every day to impact people around us as well.

Fleming was a poor Scottish farmer. One day, while trying to make a living for his family, he heard a cry for help coming from a nearby bog. He dropped his tools and ran to the bog. There, mired to his waist in black muck, was a terrified boy, screaming and struggling to free himself. Farmer Fleming saved the lad from what could have been a slow and terrifying death.

The next day, a fancy carriage pulled up to the Scotsman's sparse surroundings. An elegantly dressed nobleman stepped out and introduced himself as the father of the boy Farmer Fleming had saved. "I want to repay you," said the nobleman. "You saved my son's life."

"No, I can't accept payment for what I did," the Scottish farmer replied, waving off the offer. At that moment, the farmer's own son came to the door of the family hovel. "Is that your son?" the nobleman asked.

"Yes," the farmer replied proudly.

"I'll make you a deal. Let me provide him with the level of education my own son will enjoy. If the lad is anything like his father, he'll no doubt grow to be a man we both will be proud of." And that he did.

Farmer Fleming's son attended the very best schools, graduated from St. Mary's Hospital Medical School in London, and went on to become known throughout the world as the noted Sir Alexander Fleming, the discoverer of penicillin.

Years afterward, the same nobleman's son who was saved from the bog was stricken with pneumonia. What saved his life this time? Penicillin. The name of the nobleman? Lord Randolph Churchill. His son's name? Sir Winston Churchill.

When you reflect on those people who have been influential in your life, if you had to distill down in one word what they were able to do, that word would be connect. Fleming and Churchill formed an emotional connection as fathers and appreciative human beings. Being influential means you are able to connect as a human. You don't have to complicate the power of influence. The people who make the most impact reflect simple, basic attributes of being human.

We've all seen the opposite, those who try to rule or force or wield power. Threatening or coercing is NOT influence. Coming from one's own self-interests or the "what's-in-it-for-me" attitude also is not true influence. This attitude does not exist in the influential person's repertoire. They give, lead, and act based on what is for the betterment of the person, team, organization, or community. They are "big picture" kind of people and can see the forest along with the trees.

Becoming influential, the *missing piece to influence,* is about getting back to the basics of human nature and common sense, and understanding that you can work on your Seven Influence Traits® to increase your level of influence. First you must know where you stand and that is where the KII® comes in. The assessment measures your level of each influence trait so you have a benchmark to launch from. Then working with me or a KII® Certified Professional allows you to focus on the traits needing upleveling. I have created programs, materials and exercises for each trait and competency which my clients have all used to increase their level of influence in their work, career, organizations and home success.

That's what it boils down to – feeling your best every day at home and at work. You want to do work that inspires you and you want your life to have meaning. We are not all Mother Teresa or Steve Jobs or whoever you hold in high regard on the influence scale, but we all, every one of us, has the potential to be influential and to reap greater satisfaction from each and every interaction.

Let go of what you thought you knew about influence and put your focus on becoming influential. There is nothing you have to do, you just simply have to BE. That is the missing piece. Your influence potential is bursting forth and it is time to discover where you need to develop your influence traits -- these traits you have known about all your life. Confidence. Commitment. Courage. Passion. Empowering. Trustworthiness. Likeability. You may take the assessment and be surprised at your results, or you may find yourself nodding that it all makes sense. Even if you never take the KII® you now have a greater understanding of how to step into the new paradigm of being influential. I trust the information shared here has given you a new way to operate and to be a better leader, no matter what positon or job title you hold.

My work (and the coaches who partner with me) includes the assessment tool to measure influence potential and then how to grow and strengthen influence and build an influence culture. One executive likened the KII® as the "Fitbit of Influence." Our research-based testing and coaching has helped hundreds of clients stand out against their competition and experience long-term success.

I invite you to take the KII® for free at www.karen-keller.com. (If you are a coach, consultant or trainer, you can become a KII® Certified Professional to use the KII® assessment and coaching materials and programs to expand the level of influence of your clients.)

If there is one thing you can do to increase your personal success and that of your organization, it is to become more influential. The returns are exponential and immeasurable. Except of course when you look at things like employee retention and profit.

It's time to leverage and maximize your impact and create a lasting legacy of success. It's time to become your influential self.

I thank you for reading.

Dr. Karen Keller

Chapter Twelve Checklist

- ☐ Influential people know that focus is a key ingredient to success.

- ☐ The best ideas come from solving common problems.

- ☐ Discover the benchmark of your influence potential.

- ☐ Effective influencers influence because of who they are.

- ☐ Your Seven Influence Traits® are used everywhere in your life.

- ☐ You have the choice to influence yourself or not.

- ☐ One never knows the impact or influence they will have on another person immediately or years later.

Acknowledgements

As a net is made up of a series of ties,
so everything in this world is connected
by a series of ties. If anyone thinks that
the mesh of a net is an independent,
isolated thing he is mistaken. It is called
a net because it is made up of a series
of interconnected meshes, and each
mesh has its place and responsibility in
relation to other meshes.

- BUDDHA

There is no way I could separate the writing of this book from the living of my life. I am remembering all the remarkable people who influenced me through their faith in me, their encouraging words, and their inspiring presence.

I have had many colleagues and clients who have taught me the satisfaction of an idea born out of the need to solve a problem or inspire movement. I would like to thank all of my coaching clients. I have been fortunate enough to coach many great leaders, enterprising teams, and motivated individuals over the last twenty years. I have learned from all of them.

For their enduring grace, perseverance, and generosity, I thank those who contributed to the realization of my book. My book editor, Kelly Epperson, who devoted her talent, inspiring ways of helping me put my words on paper, and her settling encouragement that kept me from getting lost in my ideas. I thank Divya Parekh who helped me realize that writing a book was more than a dream. She helped me make it a reality. I'd also like to thank my team who has been with me for many years; Kelly Johnson, Zachary Cole, Brittney Owens, and Deborah Miller. Their designs, editing, reading, ideas, and suggestions were invaluable. But even more valuable is their loyalty, commitment, courage, and passion in all the work they do.

I would like to thank my family. My husband, Randy, for his unconditional and reassuring support that kept me going even when I thought having a root canal would be easier. My two daughters, Beth and Megan, for their ideas, and staying true to their authentic compass.

Finally, I'd like to thank you for choosing my book to read. My wish is that *Influence* has helped bring the success of your journey just a little bit closer.

Sometimes it's the very people who no one imagines anything of who do things that no one can imagine.

- DR. ALAN TURING
English computer scientist & mathematician

Learn More

For more information on the research and development
behind the Keller Influence Indicator® (KII®), please visit:

www.Karen-Keller.com/kii/research-summary-report

To learn more about Dr. Keller's workbooks,
programs and training, go to:

www.Karen-Keller.com/products

To find out your Influence Potential on the
Commitment scale, take a free trial KII® Assessment at:

www.karen-keller.com/kii/take-the-kii

Keller Influence Institute

Continue your influence growth and development at Keller Influence Institute.

- Measure your Influence Potential
- Maximize your influence strengths
- Eliminate your influence challenges
- Increase your market share and competitive advantage
- Build an influence culture

Visit Karen-Keller.com today!

Or, for a consultation call with Dr. Keller please email
info@Karen-Keller.com

KII® Assessment – KII® Report – SOCR™ Report

Take the KII® Assessment and discover YOUR EXACT SCORE on each of the Seven Influence Traits®. KII® Report provides detailed information on each trait and how you can improve. The SOCR™ Report illustrates how you show up, based on the Seven Influence Traits® scores, as a leader, communicator, team member, strategist, and executor.

KII® Trait Workbooks

Get the KII® Workbooks to continue your growth and development in building a strong influence foundation. Each KII® Workbook contains three levels of development (Fundamentals, Competencies, and Mastery) for each of the Seven Influence Traits® with step-by-step guides, exercises, lesson plans and additional information. Workbooks can be used as a self-study course or with a KII® Certified Coach. Please visit: **www.Karen-Keller.com/products**

Building an Influence Culture™ Program

Want to develop the influence strengths of your employees, teams, and executives? The Building an Influence Culture™ Program is instrumental in assisting organizations in knowing where to invest in their High Potentials, how to identify and develop emerging leaders, and how to build a solid organizational infrastructure (culture) grounded in influence. Please visit: **www.Karen-Keller.com/products**

For more information, products, and trainings, please visit: **www.Karen-Keller.com**

If you are a coach or consultant, we offer trainings and certification to use the KII® assessment and program! Please visit: **www.Karen-Keller.com**

Index

belonging, sense of, 175
benchmark, of influence potential, 186–187. *See also* Seven Influence Traits®
Berger, Jonah, 43–44
Blanchard, Ken, 89
body language, 129
brands
    organizational, 86
    self, 87, 148
Burns, Ursula, 132
businesses. *See* organizations

C

capital, human, 70, 82–83, 144–146
career. See jobs
Carnegie, Dale, 12–13, 183
certainty, 57–58, 76, 90
changes
    as need, personal, 58–59, 90–91
    vs shifts, 17–19
coaching up, 10
collaboration, 26, 40, 43–45, 76–77
Colonel Sanders, 132
commitment
    about, 103
    author's, 131
    checklist for, 119
    examples of, 132, 134
    and focus, 181, 182
    low, 103–104, 139
    and team effectiveness, 157–159
communication, as a competency, 155–157
community. *See* relationships
companies. *See* organizations

expectations, from others, 143

F
failures, 46, 185
fear, 152, 156–157. See also courage
fear of missing out (FOMO), 152
Fernando, Antony, 1
Fisher, Carl, 113
focus, 106, 179–182
FOMO (fear of missing out), 152
friendships, 12–13, 48, 60. See also relationships

G
Gable, Clark, 3
Gerstner, Lou, 30
global marketplaces, 86
Goethe, Johan Wolfgang von, 146
gossip, 158
growth
    career, 45–47, 77–78
    as personal need, 61, 92–93

H
hamster wheel, 152
hard work, 26
Hawkins, Jeff, 57–58
Hill, Napoleon, 128
Home for the Children, 2
honesty. See trustworthiness
How to Win Friends and Influence People (Carnegie), 12–13, 183
human capital, 70, 82–83, 144–146
human nature, 43, 167
Human Needs Psychology, 57

I

identity, of employees, 82–87, 184–185, 192
importance, feeling of, 59–60, 77–78, 91
importance vs urgency, 69–70
independence, of employees, 29, 32, 163
indifference, 103, 106–107
influence. *See also* other influence headings
    definition of, 7
    doing vs being (*See* influential, being)
    industry, 11
    and intention, 84–85
    and meaning, 84–85
    self, 117
    traditional methods of, 13
    traits (*See* Seven Influence Traits®)
    transition from (*See* transitions, influence to
    influential, being)
    types of, 11
influential, being. *See also* other influence headings
    ability of, 168–170, 172–175
    about, 14–17
    assessing, 187 (*See also* Keller Influence Indicator® (KII®))
    employee's, developing (*See* development, of
    employees)
    and identity, 82–87, 184–185, 192
    impact of, 190–192
    vs influence, 6–9, 10–11, 14–17, 15–16, 141
    prevalence of, 146–148
    and self-view (*See* self-view, and influential, being)
    transition to (*See* transitions, influence to influential,
    being)
    voice of, 140–143
influential potential. *See also other influence headings*

knowledge, 61

L

Lasseter, John, 24, 28
leadership
    benefits of, 34
    as a competency, 153–158
    and employees' needs, 76–77
    foundation of, 12
    and growth of employees, 47
    ineffective, 33–34, 138–139, 157–158
    and micromanagement, 31–33, 49, 162
    pressures of, 152–153, 153–154
    and relationship, with employees, 49–50
    servant, 62
    and trust, 40
lies. *See* truth
likeability
    about, 110
    checklist for, 124
    and execution, 162–163
    low, 110–111
Lincoln, Abraham, 64
listening, 128–129
love, as personal need, 60–61, 92, 175. *See also* relationships

M

management. *See* leadership
marketing industry, 10
Maslow, Abraham, 57
meaning, 84–85
measurement, of influence potential, 186. *See also* Keller Influence Indicator® (KII®)
meditation, 180–181

pressures, of employees, 151–153
problem solving, 30–35, 113–115. *See also* problems, in organizations
problems, in organizations
    engagement, lack of, 33
    ignored, 30
    leadership, 33–34
    micromanagement, 31–33, 49, 162
    relationships, of co-workers, 49–50
    slackers, 30–31
processes, internal, 15
productivity, 25–26, 30–32
profit, 41, 86, 112, 142–143
psychological influence. *See* influence
purpose, 62, 84, 103, 182. *See* also passion

Q
questioning (asking why), 87–88

R
real influence. *See* influential, being
recognition, of employees, 41–43, 91, 145–146
recruitment, 42, 73–74
relationships
    emotional, 16
    friends, making, 12–13, 49–50, 60
    and influential potential, 183
    as need, personal, 60–61, 92, 175
    in workplace, 48–50, 60, 89, 110
reputation, 15, 87, 148, 183
resolution, 137–138
result-driven, 162–163
retention, of employees, 42, 60
return on investment (ROI), 41

www.ingramcontent.com/pod-product-compliance
Lightning Source LLC
Chambersburg PA
CBHW031500180326
41458CB00044B/6650/J